ST. LOUIS AND THE GREAT WAR

S. PATRICK ALLIE

T0385442

Missouri Historical Society Press
St. Louis
Distributed by University of Chicago Press

SPECIAL THANKS TO THE CRAWFORD TAYLOR FOUNDATION AND THE TAYLOR FAMILY

Library of Congress Cataloging-in-Publication Data
Names: Allie, S. Patrick, author. | Missouri History Museum, issuing body.
Title: St. Louis and the Great War / S. Patrick Allie.
Description: St. Louis, MO : Missouri Historical Society Press, [2018] |
Includes bibliographical references.
Identifiers: LCCN 2018029778 | ISBN 9781883982942 (pbk. : alk. paper)
Subjects: LCSH: World War, 1914-1918--Missouri--Saint Louis--Exhibitions. | World War, 1914-1918-
-War work--Missouri--Saint Louis--Exhibitions. |Missouri History Museum--Catalogs. | Saint Louis
(Mo.)--History--20th century--Exhibitions.
Classification: LCC D570.85.M8 A44 2018 | DDC 940.3/77866--dc23
LC record available at https://lccn.loc.gov/2018029778

Cover image: 89th Division passing through the Court of Honor, 1919, Missouri Historical
Society Collections, P0821-01-304
Cover and interior design by Sarah Hackman
Distributed by University of Chicago Press
Printed and bound in the United States by Sheridan Books, Inc.

TABLE OF CONTENTS

INTRODUCTION

AMERICAN INVOLVEMENT IN A GLOBAL WAR was never intended to happen. At no time was that clearer than during the 1916 Democratic National Convention held in St. Louis, where incumbent Woodrow Wilson was nominated as the party's presidential candidate under the slogan "He Kept Us Out of War." The general nationwide preference for neutrality led to Wilson's reelection as president in November 1916, yet by April 1917 he was standing before Congress asking for a declaration of war against Germany.

Over the course of 20 months, until armistice was declared in November 1918, the United States transitioned from an isolationist nation to a major player on the world stage. Communities throughout the country came together like never before in support of the war effort. Americans from every walk of life enlisted in the military, joined service organizations such as the American Red Cross or YMCA, took on jobs at factories and farms, and donated what they could.

In Missouri more than 760,000 men expressed their willingness to make the world "safe for democracy" by registering for the draft, including thousands of African Americans. Of the 77,000 Missourians drafted, more than 9,000 were black. Many were assigned to labor and stevedore units overseas as part of a segregated military, but some served as members of the 92nd and 93rd Infantry Divisions—the only African American combat units. These soldiers fought with distinction in France, but they did so as part of the French army because white Americans refused to fight alongside them.

Women played a significant role in the war as well. In Missouri many of the women who participated in the famous 1916 Golden Lane demonstration in support of women's suffrage began working in factories, entering military service, and organizing initiatives on the home front. At the Wagner Electric Company in Wellston, Missouri, a quarter of the company's wartime workforce was women. Female nurses from St. Louis served with their fellow Washington University students and faculty members at Base Hospital 21 in Rouen, France, pioneering the use of X-rays, treating thousands of injured soldiers, and launching the early study and treatment of "war neurosis" (known today as PTSD, or post-traumatic stress disorder). At the state, county, and city levels, the Women's Committee of the Missouri Council of Defense ensured ongoing support of the war effort through "patriotic education" about food conservation, war-savings thrift stamps, and the enemy.

Sometimes that enemy seemed closer at hand, particularly in St. Louis, where one out of every five residents was a first- or second-generation German immigrant. Backlash against Germans was pervasive during wartime. Schoolchildren were no longer taught how to speak German; German-language newspapers were censored; and German companies, such as Anheuser-Busch, were scrutinized for their foreign ties. In perhaps the most horrific chapter of anti-German hostility both locally and nationally, immigrant Robert Prager was lynched in Collinsville, Illinois, on unfounded accusations of being a spy.

In the years since all of this took place, World War I—the supposed War to End All Wars—has been overshadowed in public perception by the war that followed it less than two decades after Germany's defeat, yet its influence across the globe endures. Both World War II and more recent conflicts have roots in World War I, from the reparations Germany was forced to pay that bankrupted the country and allowed for the rise of the Nazi Party, to the dissection of the Ottoman Empire that has led to decades of war in the Middle East. That influence reaches close to home too. Having experienced a progressive France and a taste of equality, black servicemen brought those ideas back to a segregated America, forming what would become the civil rights movement. Similarly, women leveraged their war work to earn the right to vote, which was granted with the passage of the 19th Amendment in 1920, just as many were returning from overseas.

These stories and more, many of which have connections to the World War I collections of the Missouri Historical Society, form the basis of this companion to the exhibit *World War I: St. Louis and the Great War* on view at the Soldiers Memorial Military Museum in downtown St. Louis. Over the years I spent surveying and cataloging World War I artifacts to prepare for this exhibit, I uncovered captivating stories about St. Louis and its citizens. These narratives are not only representative of America's experience during World War I, but they also provide a view of the Great War through the unique lens of St. Louis, a city that still bears the marks of a turbulent time, though some have faded a century later.

Through this book you'll discover World War I's lasting legacy in St. Louis, as well as St. Louisans' impact on the war on the front lines and on the home front. The next time you pass by Pershing Ave., you'll know that the street was once called Berlin Ave. but was renamed for the famous Missouri military hero as a result of anti-German backlash. When you drive down Kingshighway Blvd., you'll be able to envision a median that was once filled with more than 1,000 brass markers alongside rows of European sycamore trees, all placed there to honor the St. Louisans who made the ultimate sacrifice in the Great War. You'll also meet courageous men and women, such as Medal of Honor recipient Captain Alexander Skinker, who ran into enemy fire to save his men, and Nurse Julia Stimson, who joined the Army Nurse Corps as chief nurse of Base Hospital 21 and later became chief nurse of the entire American Expeditionary Force.

In the following pages, my hope is that you'll learn something new about St. Louis and how it changed—and was changed by—the Great War.

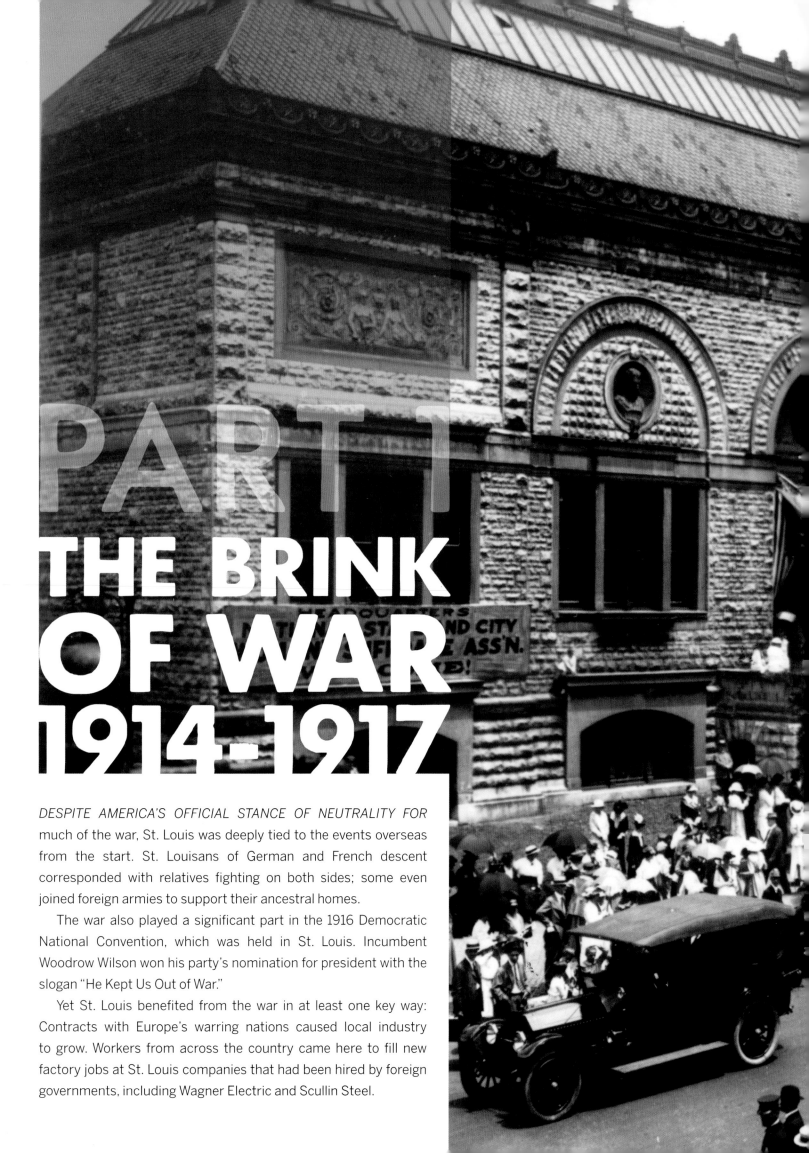

PART 1
THE BRINK OF WAR 1914-1917

DESPITE AMERICA'S OFFICIAL STANCE OF NEUTRALITY FOR much of the war, St. Louis was deeply tied to the events overseas from the start. St. Louisans of German and French descent corresponded with relatives fighting on both sides; some even joined foreign armies to support their ancestral homes.

The war also played a significant part in the 1916 Democratic National Convention, which was held in St. Louis. Incumbent Woodrow Wilson won his party's nomination for president with the slogan "He Kept Us Out of War."

Yet St. Louis benefited from the war in at least one key way: Contracts with Europe's warring nations caused local industry to grow. Workers from across the country came here to fill new factory jobs at St. Louis companies that had been hired by foreign governments, including Wagner Electric and Scullin Steel.

▲ **Votes for Women button, ca. 1915**
Missouri Historical Society Collections
2009-159-0001

◄ **Unidentified suffragist wearing a Votes for Women sash, June 1916**
Missouri Historical Society Collections
N39082

➤ **President Woodrow Wilson, ca. 1918**
Library of Congress
LC-D416-83

▼ **Democratic National Convention ticket, 1916**
Missouri Historical Society Collections
D02399_0003, D02399_0002

ST. LOUIS HOSTS THE 1916 DEMOCRATIC NATIONAL CONVENTION

As the 1916 presidential election approached, sitting president Woodrow Wilson was riding a wave of public approval built on his negotiations with Germany to halt attacks on American merchant ships and maintain peace. Running with the slogan "He Kept Us Out of War," Wilson received his party's nomination during the Democratic National Convention held in St. Louis.

Though he was successful in maintaining neutrality abroad, Wilson faced a growing fight at home from the women's suffrage movement. During the same convention where he was nominated, hundreds of women wearing gold sashes emblazoned with the words "Votes for Women" made their voices heard by forming a "Golden Lane" along the route that convention attendees took to get from their hotel to the Coliseum.

Wanted! 10,000 Women Recruits!

IF { You believe in Woman Suffrage.
You believe that woman's vote can help your country, city, home, your children or yourself.

Enlist NOW!

Women from every State from Maine to California are coming to St. Louis to take part in a great Suffrage Demonstration, which will take place on the first day of the

National Democratic Convention

Elsewhere women have paraded; but here the parade will be **"WALKLESS"**. A mile of Suffragists, dressed in white and bearing the suffrage yellow, will stand shoulder to shoulder in a straight line, which will form a

GOLDEN LANE on LOCUST STREET
between the JEFFERSON HOTEL and the COLISEUM
FROM 10 a. m. UNTIL 12 NOON. On JUNE 14th.

Help us make this demonstration so big and beautiful that Missouri will be proud of its women and that the delegates to the convention can not fail to feel the force of the plea for

VOTES FOR WOMEN
It May Mean a Suffrage Plank in the National Platform!
Every Woman Counts!   We Need You!

Sign the attached slip and send or bring it at once to

SUFFRAGE HEADQUARTERS, F-19 Railway Exchange Building

People from out of the city wishing to make hotel or boarding house reservations, please communicate with Mrs. Chas. Passmore, Suffrage Headquarters, Railway Exchange Building, St. Louis.

I will take part in the Suffrage Demonstration on June 14th.

Name————————————

Address————————————

Ward————— Phone Number—————

▲ Democratic National Convention in St. Louis, June 1916
Library of Congress
LC-B2-3888-5

➤ Woodrow Wilson campaign button, 1916
Missouri Historical Society Collections
X00585

◀ *Missouri Woman* ad to recruit Golden Lane
participants, May 1916
Missouri Historical Society Collections
N23856

▼ Woodrow Wilson and Missouri senator James Reed
campaign button, 1916
Missouri Historical Society Collections
X08714

THE PUNITIVE EXPEDITION, 1916

On January 11, 1916, six years of ongoing conflict and frail diplomatic relations between the United States and Mexico climaxed with Mexican revolutionary Pancho Villa's raid on the southern border town of Columbus, New Mexico. Villa's attack caused the deaths of 10 civilians and 8 soldiers. Missouri National Guardsmen, including many St. Louisans, were part of a surge of American troops sent to defend the border in the following days.

Two months later Missouri native Gen. John Pershing led a force of 6,675 men into Mexico in pursuit of Villa. The expedition failed to capture Villa, but it did provide Pershing with invaluable experience in the use of new military technologies such as airplanes, motorized vehicles, and machine guns.

∧ Gen. Pershing (center) inspecting camp during the Punitive Expedition, 1916
Library of Congress
LC-USZ62-89220

∨ Mexican Border Service Medal of Mus. Edward W. Burkhardt, ca. 1916
Soldiers Memorial Military Museum Collections
SM1968-004-0007

< US Army military campaign hat, ca. 1916
Missouri Historical Society Collections
1994-029-0004

1887   Oliver Vie   1918
Pvt. 1cl. Co.K 26th Inf.

PRIVATE OLIVER VIE, COMPANY K, 26TH INFANTRY, 1ST DIVISION

"it was 115 in the shade yesterday the place is full of snakes and wolfs and mosquites the wolfs howl all night and keep us awake why i would live in this god for saken place for no money if the mexicans dont kill us i guess the heat will . . ."—Pvt. Oliver Vie to his sister, Grace Ashton, in St. Louis

Born and raised on the north side of St. Louis, Oliver "Ollie" Vie joined the US Army in 1913. He spent the next four years on the Mexican border protecting vital sites from Mexican bandits. Pvt. Vie regularly wrote to his family in St. Louis about the harsh weather in Mexico and clashes with Mexican bandits.

When the United States entered World War I in 1917, Vie became part of the 1st Infantry Division. Because he was among the first contingent of American troops sent to France, Vie fought in some of the earliest American engagements of the war, including the July 1918 Battle of Soissons. This was a crucial victory for the Allies that allowed them to reclaim gains the Germans had made earlier that year.

Pvt. Vie was seriously injured at Soissons and died from his wounds on July 20, 1918.

‹ Pvt. Oliver Vie, ca. 1917
Missouri Historical Society Collections
P0159-00480

NEUTRALITY AND PREPAREDNESS

America was a split country in 1914. Many supported President Wilson's stance of strict neutrality and avoidance of any military buildup that would signal possible American involvement in the war. Others believed the United States was vulnerable and needed to bolster its military.

The Preparedness Movement gained traction as the war in Europe continued to grow. Throughout 1915 and 1916, former president Theodore Roosevelt toured the country speaking on preparedness and universal military service. Roosevelt stopped in St. Louis on May 31, 1916. Three days later, a parade was held here to "demonstrate in a successful manner the overwhelming sentiment of the citizens of St. Louis in favor of Preparedness."

› Preparedness Parade flyer, 1916
Missouri Historical Society Collections
A1771-00007

SAINT LOUIS
Citizens' Preparedness Parade
NON-PARTISAN—PATRIOTIC
National Preparedness Day, Saturday, June 3d

A great citizens' parade in favor of Preparedness will be held on June 3rd under the auspices of the St. Louis Branch of the National Security League, and will be reviewed by Governor Major and Mayor Kiel. More than fifty-six organizations and sixty trades have already signified their intention of taking part.

The object of the parade is to demonstrate in a successful manner the overwhelming sentiment of the citizens of St. Louis in favor of Preparedness.

INVITATION.

Every individual, every school, every business house, and every organization—civic, religious, educational, labor, commercial, fraternal and military, is invited.

GROUPS.

Business houses in the same line will be grouped together in the march; e. g., boots and shoes, dry goods, etc. Any business house which can muster one hundred or more men may carry its own banner.

Organizations will be grouped according to character of organization; e. g., fraternal, labor, etc. Each should carry its own banner stating that it is for Preparedness.

Individuals not belonging to any business house or organization represented, are urged to form into groups and march, or to join some group already organized.

SUGGESTION.

Each marcher should carry a small American flag.

IMPORTANT.

Notify, either by telephone or letter, the office of the National Security League, 403 LaSalle Bldg., Olive 4077, on or before Tuesday, May 30th:

1st. Name and address of leader.
2nd. Number of men in group.

LINE OF MARCH.

Parade will form at 12th and Market Sts. Will proceed thence on 12th to Locust, out Locust to Channing, thence west on Lindell to Vandeventer Ave. The parade will start promptly at 1:30 p. m.

You will be notified in the newspapers where your group will assemble and the time at which you will march.

BANDS.

Union Bands will be provided by the Committee.

The appeal is made to citizens for decorations on buildings and residences throughout the city, particularly along the line of march. Every flag-pole should fly the flag. Decorations for the parade will serve for the convention. 70

"'Neutrality' is a negative word. It is a word that does not express what America ought to feel. . . . We are not trying to keep out of trouble; we are trying to preserve the foundations upon which peace can be rebuilt."
—President Woodrow Wilson, speaking to the Daughters of the American Revolution on October 11, 1915

"I am not asking you to let the other fellow prepare that he may do your fighting for you. I am asking you to prepare, you yourselves; all of us here; all Americans everywhere."—Former president Theodore Roosevelt, speaking in St. Louis on May 31, 1916

St. Louis has long been a city of immigrants, many with European ties. As war raged in Europe, the question for local immigrants was whether to be loyal to their ancestral country or their adopted one. President Wilson recognized these divided loyalties and knew the war would only add more tension to the mix. The chief advocate of neutrality, Wilson hoped to position America as a postwar peacemaker.

⌃ Preparedness Parade, June 1916
Missouri Historical Society Collections
P0095-00004

⌃ American Neutrality League ribbon, ca. 1916
Missouri Historical Society Collections
X09875

ST. LOUIS'S GERMAN TIES

At the turn of the century, the United States was a melting pot of immigrants and cultures. In 1910, 2 out of every 10 St. Louisans were either born in Germany or had parents who were born in Germany. German clubs and religious organizations, including Turners and Lutherans, were especially prominent in the city. St. Louis Germans closely followed news of the war obtained through German-language newspapers and correspondence with their German relatives.

22. 9. 1914

Dear Cousin,

As you know we are in war. I am now in France near Reims. We are astonished that France and Russia could begin a war with such troops. The french artillerie is very well drilled. But that's all.

I was at first at the german frontier (—belgium) with my squadron to guard the arrival of the troops and had there heavy fights with the francitineurs. As these reported the french governement had sent man with money, military rifles and ammunition. The people even wifes shot from behind out of windows, trees, walls, cellars etc. I saw a wife, which gave a glass of milk to a medecine and another me cut his throat with a razor when he drunk. So i I could tell you many histories of cruelty. We were obliged to bring all these before a court martial.

DEAR COUSIN!

In 1914 and 1915, St. Louisan Mary Clemens corresponded with Fritz Von Versen, her German cousin and a captain in the German cavalry. Von Versen, like many of his countrymen, was thrilled about the prospect of war and assured of German military superiority.

Dear Cousin! As you know we are in war. I am in France near Reims. We are astonished that France and Russia could begin a war with such troops. The french artilleries is very well drilled. But that's all. I was at first at its german belgium frontier with my squadron to guard the arrival of the troops and had there heavy fights with the frontireurs [francs-tiereurs]. As these reported the french government has sent man with money, military rifles and munition. The people even wifes shot from behind out of windows, trees, walls, cellars etc. I saw wife which gave a glass of milk to a medic and another one cut his throat with a rasor when he drink. So, I could tell you many histories of cruelty. We were obliged to bring all these before a court martial.
—Fritz Von Versen to Mary Clemens, September 22, 1914

Von Versen was also very critical of the French colonial troops and the Russian army.

It is incredible that Christian nations brought to Europe such wild tribes. They have very few military values and murder all wounded men. . . . The colored men make much noise and wild gestures. . . .

[Continued in the same letter]

The Russians have plenty of men but these are very fearful and stupid. The patrols are never less than 30 men. The Kosacks are no soldiers, only murders and robbers. They behaved in germany like the soldiers some hundred years ago. Even the Russians fear them. In Germany they treated dreadfully the wifes and girls and killed and burnt all. Therefore they are killed where we can and we gave them never pardon especial as they kill ever prisoner cruelly since the begin of the war, theyfore always glad if they are prisoner. The russian people don't like the war and to fight. . . .
—Fritz Von Versen to Mary Clemens, January 20, 1915

◀ ▶ Letter from German army officer Fritz Von Versen to Mary Clemens, September 1914
Missouri Historical Society Collections
A0298-00013

GERMAN NEWSPAPERS

St. Louis's large first- and second-generation German communities got their news from several German-language newspapers, the largest of which was the *Westliche Post*. Staunchly pro-German and supportive of American neutrality, the paper took particular issue with the selling of war matériel and other military aid to the Allies and gave expanded coverage to anti-war protests and the American Neutrality League.

∧ *Westliche Post* **building at Broadway and Market, ca. 1950**

Missouri Historical Society Collections
N02059

ST. LOUIS SUPPORTS AND SUPPLIES THE WAR IN EUROPE, 1914–1917

Although the United States was diplomatically neutral, that didn't prevent American citizens from giving money to war-related causes or producing war goods for Europe. Foreign war bonds were sold in banks across the city for all the belligerent nations, including Germany. Believing America would remain neutral, St. Louis brewer August Busch and his mother purchased $500,000 in German war bonds through the St. Louis Union Trust Company.

St. Louis dollars also went overseas to aid the war's displaced civilian population and wounded. Fundraisers were widespread, including war-relief bazaars to solicit money for food and supplies for European civilians. Meanwhile, companies across St. Louis churned out war matériel for Great Britain, France, and Russia.

⌃ **Close-up view of shells outside of Wagner Electric, ca. 1916**
Missouri Historical Society Collections
P0244-K0656

⌃ St. Louis War Relief Bazaar armband, 1915
Missouri Historical Society Collections
X13618_0002, X13618_0003

⌐ French War Orphans medal, ca. 1916
Missouri Historical Society Collections
X09931

⌄ American Fund for French Wounded pin, ca. 1916
Missouri Historical Society Collections
X09953

CAN'T STAY OUT OF THE FIGHT

Whether driven by adventure, duty, or a sense of inevitability, hundreds of Americans joined foreign armies between 1915 and 1917, including St. Louisan Charles Chouteau Johnson. He joined the French Foreign Legion and eventually became part of the famed Lafayette Escadrille, a French fighter squadron that was largely composed of Americans.

⌃ **Lt. Charles Chouteau Johnson with the Lafayette Escadrille at the Battle of Verdun, 1916**
Missouri Historical Society Collections
N18282

Among America's World War I ambulance drivers—including well-known figures Walt Disney and Ernest Hemingway—was Central West End resident Joseph Garneau Weld. In October 1916 he joined the American Field Service, a French ambulance corps composed of Americans. Pvt. Weld was with the American Field Service for nine months, until the United States joined the war and he was transferred to the US Army. During his time overseas, Weld collected the insignia of enemy combatants, attaching them to souvenir "hate belts."

⌃ **French M2 gas mask carrier of Pvt. Joseph Garneau Weld, inscribed with battles and sectors he served in, ca. 1916**
Missouri Historical Society Collections
1919-075-0014

‹ **Hate belt of Pvt. Joseph Garneau Weld, ca. 1916**
Missouri Historical Society Collections
1919-075-0035

› **Pvt. Joseph Garneau Weld, ca. 1918**
Missouri Historical Society Collections
P0649-00010

LIEUTENANT JOSEPH DESLOGE, FRENCH 11TH FIELD ARTILLERY

Proud of his French heritage and fluent in the language, St. Louisan Joseph Desloge was drawn to the defense of his ancestral country. He joined a French ambulance company in January 1917 and enlisted in the French Foreign Legion three months later. Desloge was commissioned as a 2nd Lieutenant in the French 11th Field Artillery Regiment, serving as a liaison officer between the French and American armies.

   During the Allied offensive in the fall of 1918, Lt. Desloge was responsible for forward communications of the artillery installed near Vouziers, France. He distinguished himself during the battle and was cited for his bravery. After the war, Desloge returned to St. Louis and built a French-style chateau in north St. Louis County named Vouziers, after the location of his World War I triumph.

◄ ⌃ **French 11th Field Artillery uniform of Lt. Joseph Desloge, ca. 1916**
Missouri Historical Society Collections
2014-079-0001

◄ **Lt. Joseph Desloge's French foreign identity booklet, ca. 1916**
Missouri Historical Society Collections
A0380-00005

THE PATH TO WAR: BELGIAN ATROCITIES, SUBMARINE WARFARE, AND A SECRET TELEGRAM

Following the outbreak of the war in August 1914, the Allied nations of France, Great Britain, and Russia sought America as an ally in the fight against Germany. Frequent reports of German atrocities in occupied Belgium, the sinking of the passenger ship *Lusitania*, and attacks on American merchant vessels pushed US relations with Germany to a breaking point and edged America closer to war.

On August 4, 1914, Germany invaded Belgium, violating that country's neutrality and bringing Great Britain into the war. Immediately afterward, the German army was accused of executing Belgian civilians, burning libraries and homes, and engaging in widespread looting. These accusations, though largely unfounded, were used as propaganda in the United States to garner support for entering the war. In response to such stories of German atrocities, including the murder of babies, St. Louisans contributed to the Belgian Relief Fund.

⌄ Belgian Relief Fund corsage, ca. 1916
Missouri Historical Society Collections
1974-013-0005

"BELGIAN BABIES"

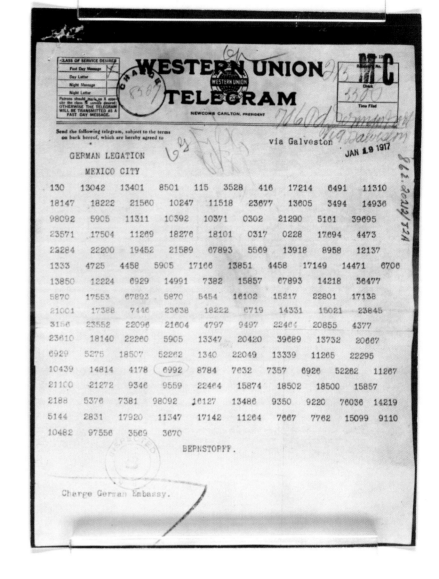

∧ **Satirical *Lusitania* medal, ca. 1916**
Missouri Historical Society Collections
1921-016-0001

∧ **Reverse side of satirical *Lusitania* medal, ca. 1916**
Missouri Historical Society Collections
1921-016-0001

➤ **Zimmermann telegram as received by the German ambassador to Mexico, January 1917**
National Archives and Records Administration
302025

On May 7, 1915, a German submarine stationed off the coast of Ireland fired its torpedoes. They hit the RMS *Lusitania*, which was en route to Liverpool, England, from New York City, and ultimately sank the ship. The attack claimed the lives of 1,191 passengers—including 159 Americans—and sparked outrage in the United States.

Erich Ralph von Gersdorff, a St. Louis mining engineer and German army reservist, was arrested under suspicion of espionage: He had been found with two telegrams warning a friend not to travel on the *Lusitania* because it was carrying armaments.

On March 3, 1917, the front page of the *St. Louis Post-Dispatch* confirmed what many had suspected: Germany was actively plotting against the United States.

Two months earlier, British intelligence officers had intercepted and deciphered a telegram from German foreign secretary Arthur Zimmermann to the German ambassador to Mexico. The telegram outlined an offer of financial aid and a promise to restore lost territory in the United States if Mexico sided with Germany in the event of an American-German conflict. Within weeks of the announcement, President Wilson urged Congress to declare war.

◀ *St. Louis Post-Dispatch* front page from March 3, 1917
Missouri Historical Society Collections
GRA00244

◀ *St. Louis Post-Dispatch* front page from May 7, 1915
Missouri Historical Society Collections
WWI-Graphic-004

▶ **Speech given by US senator William Stone of Missouri regarding the arming of merchant ships, March 1917**
Missouri Historical Society Collections
A0914-00006

Congressional Record.

SIXTY-FOURTH CONGRESS, SECOND SESSION.

Vol. 54.   WASHINGTON, THURSDAY, MARCH 15, 1917.   No. 75, Part 2.

SPEECH
OF
HON. WILLIAM J. STONE,
OF MISSOURI,
IN THE SENATE OF THE UNITED STATES,

Saturday, March 3 (legislative day of Friday, March 2), 1917.

The Senate had under consideration the bill (H. R. 21052) authorizing the President of the United States to supply merchant ships, the property of citizens of the United States and bearing American registry, with defensive arms, and for other purposes.

Mr. STONE. Mr. President, I would rather trust President Wilson to keep the United States out of war than the jingoes now so prevalent and so clamorous for war in some sections of the country. I do not think these clamorers are numerically dominant in the country at large, but I am sorry to say that they appear to have become dominant in the Congress. I wish to make it plain that I am opposed to involving this country in the European war without infinitely greater provocation than we have yet had, and, without asserting it as a fact—and the President's future course will determine that—I believe the President to be in substantial sympathy with this view. Unless I am woefully mistaken, the President loves peace and wants peace more than war. I think he is sincere about that, and he is the one man in America who can do most to keep us out of war. The Congress may declare war; they can put us into war, but the President can do more than all others to keep us out of war. I believe he would rather rest his fame, as did Washington and Jefferson, on works done for the homes and happiness of his people and of mankind than to rest it, as did Cæsar and Napoleon, upon the bloody triumphs of battle fields. His devotion to peace has been demonstrated. Events in Mexico have been exasperating beyond measure. The lives and property rights of Americans have been ruthlessly sacrificed in Mexico, and brutal, costly, sanguinary crimes have been committed by Mexicans even on our side of the American frontier in the States of Texas and New Mexico. For years the President has been subjected to the strain and pressure of a tremendous clamor for war with Mexico, but instead of striking with a mailed hand he set his heart on helping, not hurting, Mexico, and therefore set his thought on peace beyond the Rio Grande. He has kept us out of war with Mexico.

And despite a weight of troubles sufficient to break the patience of almost any man, and despite the clamor, intrigues, and subterfuges resorted to to entrap him into some act of war with European powers, he has up to this time stood as firm as a rock. He has also kept us out of war in Europe. He has so far kept the peace in both Europe and America. I repeat, therefore, that I would rather trust him than all that horde of official weaklings who daily fly their kites to see which way the wind blows. Personally I have felt all through these troublous months that the President would do everything within his power that any man clothed with grave responsibility might honorably do to save this country from sharing in the dread calamity of that conflagration which is destroying Europe. He would not, as he should not, brook insolent attack on our national honor or intentional wrong against our people; but I believe he would in future as in the past bear with great patience, as he should, the burden of incidental and resultant injuries flowing out of the turbulence of a great war, but not wantonly committed in a spirit of hostility to our Government or our people.

For nearly four years I have worked by the President's side, and have enjoyed both his friendship and his confidence. He knows—yes, he is bound to know—that he holds a high place in my esteem and a warm place in my affections. I have not always agreed with him about things. Two such men as we could not always fully agree; but I have, as a rule, followed his lead and gone along with him as the titular head of my party,

85491—17126

and in close alliance doing team work with him. I know the man and believe in him. If the question to-day were one only of faith and trust in him, I would not hesitate; if it were only a question of domestic policy or even of foreign policy of lesser consequence; if it were anything, indeed, not of absolutely vital moment such as I regard the present matter to be, I would be very slow to withhold my support when the President asked it; but in this instance I profoundly regret to say that I can not vote for this bill in its present form, even though the President recommends it. This is my first disagreement with the President which we have not been able to reconcile. I am sorry for this, but it can not be helped. I can not take part in committing what I believe would be an unpardonable and perilous mistake.

I believe the bill to be not only violative of the Constitution—destructive of one of the most important powers vested in the Congress, the war-making power—but that its passage would set a precedent fraught with future danger to our form of government and to public liberty. Moreover, and aside from the question of its constitutionality, and purely as a matter of public policy, I would regard the bill with grave apprehension, as being wholly wrong in its possible, if not natural, tendencies. I would not for a moment seriously consider the question of voting such extraordinary and dangerous powers into the hands of any Executive of less poise, moral courage, and straightforwardness of purpose than President Wilson. I believe President Wilson would strive to use this power, if granted, as prudently, as justly, and as entirely for the public good as any single man amongst us all; and I would rather trust him, as I have said, to preserve the peace of these States and to aid in restoring the peace of the world than to trust the whole united conclave of turbulent jingoes, whether in or out of Congress; but I fear too much the danger of an example so pregnant of future mischief to aid in establishing it, even in circumstances calculated to inspire confidence that the power granted would not in this instance be wantonly abused, and when it might even be considered by many conservative men who love peace not to be a wholly unwise expedient for a present emergency. And here let me add that while I do not assume the province of protecting the President from sinister influences or the machinations of evil men, I think it would be most unfortunate for the President himself if the power to involve us in this European war by his own act should be confided to him. Then he would have to stand alone. I fear the Congress can no longer be relied upon as the friend of neutrality and peace; I fear the Congress has become inoculated with the poison or passion of war and stands all too ready and upon too slight provocation to render homage to the god of wrath. Still the Congress should remain unstripped of their power and responsibility, that they might still stand at least as a breakwater against the waves that otherwise would roll unhindered against the President standing alone. The plotters and intrigants of war would still be obliged to deal with the Congress as well as with the President. Isolate the President and make it possible for him by his own authorized act to inaugurate war, and instantly all manner of schemes, subterfuges, intrigues, and, I doubt not, even crimes would be resorted to to force his hand. It would be an awful responsibility for a great democracy to confide to any single man ever born of woman.

THE CONSTITUTIONALITY OF THE LAW.

I have said that an act in the language of this bill would be unconstitutional. I have heard men say in substance that they agreed with me about that, but that they intended to vote for the bill anyhow. Why? Because, they said, the President advised it, and they had faith in him. That was the philosophy of Tim Campbell, who protested that the Constitution should not be permitted to stand between friends. Adopt this Campbelltonian philosophy and you will open an easy way, as it certainly would be a very accommodating way, for construing the Constitution; but it is a way no Senator is authorized to adopt. The Constitution vests the war-making power alone in

PART 2
OVER THERE
1917-1919

"PRESIDENT PROCLAIMS WAR; GERMAN SHIPS SEIZED." THAT headline spread across the front page of the *St. Louis Post-Dispatch* on April 6, 1917, announcing the declaration of war against Germany. Accompanying headlines—including "How U.S. Plans to Train a Million Men in a Year" and "To Germans Here: Obey the Law and Keep Mouths Shut"—underscored the official end to neutrality and clearly identified the enemy.

Over the following weeks and months, one of the largest mobilization efforts undertaken in United States history began. Ultimately 2 million American service members brought hope to the war-weary Allies.

▲ **President Woodrow Wilson asking Congress to declare war, April 1917**

Library of Congress

LC-H261-29825

BUILDING AN ARMY: THE AMERICAN EXPEDITIONARY FORCE (AEF)

In April 1917 the US Army totaled 127,588 soldiers and officers—many more would be needed to fight the Central Powers. The task of building and fielding an American army presence in Europe was given to Missouri general John Pershing. Pershing eventually commanded an army of over 2 million. More than 156,000 Missourians, among them thousands of St. Louisans, were represented throughout Pershing's army.

GENERAL JOHN "BLACK JACK" PERSHING, US ARMY

John Pershing earned his "Black Jack" nickname during his service with the 10th Cavalry Regiment, better known as the Buffalo Soldiers. He also served on the American frontier during the Spanish-American War and commanded the Punitive Expedition of 1916.

On May 10, 1917, President Wilson passed over numerous senior generals to name Pershing the General of the Armies, a decision that caused the Laclede, Missouri, native to face intense scrutiny. Immediately upon taking command, Gen. Pershing was tasked with building up the US Army. He also faced pressure from French and British military and political officials to place American troops under their command, something he resisted. Ultimately, World War I made Pershing an American hero.

◄ **Gen. John Pershing, ca. 1920**
Library of Congress
LC-H823-1534

➤ **Selective Service registration questionnaire, 1917**
Missouri Historical Society Collections
A1771-00022

THE DRAFT: SELECTIVE SERVICE ACT OF 1917

Despite fears of backlash and rioting, the Wilson administration made the controversial decision to institute a national draft in order to quickly grow the military. From mid-1917 through much of 1918, all males between the ages of 18 and 45 were required to register for military service. During the war, 2.8 million of those registered men were drafted. More than 760,000 men registered for the draft in Missouri. Of those, 77,000 were drafted, including 9,219 African Americans. Missouri conscripts were represented in nearly every division raised through the draft.

BLANK FORMS

Form 1   ## REGISTRATION CARD   (**Front**)   No........................

		Age, in yrs.
1	Name in full..	
	(Given name) (Family name)	

2 Home address ....
(No.)   (Street)   (City)   (State)

3 Date of birth........................
(Month)   (Day)   (Year)

4 Are you (1) a natural-born citizen, (2) a naturalized citizen, (3) an alien, (4) or have you declared your intention (specify which)?........................

5 Where were you born?........................
(Town)   (State)   (Nation)

6 If not a citizen, of what country are you a citizen or subject?........................

7 What is your present trade, occupation, or office?........................

8 By whom employed?........................
Where employed?........................

9 Have you a father, mother, wife, child under 12, or a sister or brother under 12, solely dependent on you for support (specify which)?........................

10 Married or single (which)?........................ Race (specify which)?........................

11 What military service have you had? Rank........................; branch........................; years........................; Nation or State........................

12 Do you claim exemption from draft (specify grounds)?........................

I affirm that I have verified above answers and that they are true.

If person is of African descent, tear off this corner

....
(Signature or mark)

On back of Registration Card is
REGISTRAR'S REPORT

1 Tall, medium, or short (specify which)?........................ Slender, medium, or stout (which)?........................

2 Color of eyes?........................ Color of hair?........................? Bald?........................

3 Has person lost arm, leg, hand, foot, or both eyes, or is he otherwise disabled (specify)?........................

I certify that my answers are true, that the person registered has read his own answers, that I have witnessed his signature, and that all of his answers of which I have knowledge are true, except as follows:

....

....

....
(Signature of Registrar)

Precinct........................

City or County........................

State........................   ....
(Date of registration)

The registration is to be made on Registration Cards (like above), which will be delivered to the Chief Registrar of each precinct, who will call for same at the office of the Board of Election Commissioners, Room 120, City Hall, on Monday, June 4, 1917.

Only **ONE** person is to be registered on each card. These cards are to be carefully filled out and retained by the Registrars. After the Registration has been completed they are to be delivered to the Executive Officer of the Board of Registration for the Ward. He is the officer who signed your Commission.

■ 35

TAKE NOTICE

All male citizens between the ages of **21 and 30, inclusive,** in the United States are required to register on **JUNE 5, 1917,** under the recent Conscription Act of Congress.

The law provides severe penalty for failure to register.

The National, State and City Governments are co-operating to have a complete registration, and to apprehend any one within the age limit of 21 to 30, inclusive, who fails to register.

The place of registration for parties residing in this building is:

Patrolman _____

_____ District.

⌃ Postcard sent to Robert Terry notifying him to register for the draft, 1917
Missouri Historical Society Collections
A1609-00001

➤ Draft exemption pin, ca. 1917
Missouri Historical Society Collections
1992-113-0022

⌃ James Young's draft registration certificate, 1917

Missouri Historical Society Collections

A1771-00006

1921
September 18

St. Louis Post Dispatch.

Names of Men From St. Louis and St. Louis County Draft Districts Listed as Deserters

War Department Records Show Those Who Were Called but Who Are Not Credited With Any Service.

The names in the following list are those of men who were drafted for military service from St. Louis and St. Louis County, but who failed to serve, according to the records of the War Department, as compiled to date. At the present time they are reported and classified as "deserters" from the military service of the United States."

The War Department has found in lists previously published the names of some men classed as "deserters" who had served honorably with the colors.

The War Department announcement says:

"Actual expenses, not to exceed $50, to include reimbursement for the amount actually expended, but not to include allowance for services, will be paid to any civil officer or to any other citizen for the apprehension and delivery to military control of any one of them. If any one of them is apprehended, he should be delivered at, and reimbursement for the actual expenses incurred by the arresting officer should be claimed at the nearest army post, camp or station."

The following lists are issued by Brigadier-General Omar Bundy, commanding the Seventh Corps Area, with headquarters at Fort Crook, Neb.:

Local Board for Division No. 1, City of St. Louis.

Fred Bayran, 502 Talcott street, St. Louis (Beyran).

Albert Chartrand, Glennonville 4313 North Fourteenth street, St. Louis.

Walter E. Drews, 2135 De Sota street, St. Louis, Mo. (Drewes).

Howard L. Fleming, Broadway and Clark avenue, St. Louis; Howard S. Fleming, 6400 North Broadway, St. Louis; Howard S. Fleming, Taylor Springs, Ill.

Frank Gilbert, 653 Morin avenue, St. Louis.

Claude F. Harder, 7800 North Broadway, St. Louis (Harden, Claud Harden).

Carl A. Herring, 419 Rebecca avenue, Wilkensburg, Pa.; Frisch Hotel, East Pittsburg, Pa.; 4269 Blair avenue, St. Louis (Hering).

Edward Jackson, Granville, N. D.

John Meyers, 4813 Bulwer, St. Louis.

John Patrick Quinn, 4300 North Broadway, St. Louis.

George Rost, Gen. Del., Toledo, O.; 1924 Linton avenue, St. Louis.

John H. Schaller, 6400 North Broadway, St. Louis.

Daniel Turley, 515 Talcott street, St. Louis.

Charles William, 185 W. Broad street, Columbia, O.; 4225 North Broadway, St. Louis (Williams).

Local Board for Division No. 10, St. Louis

Harry J. Barnett, 3640 Marine avenue, St. Louis.

Mack Brown, 3640 Marine avenue, St. Louis.

Lohzow Guinn, 3640 Marine avenue, St. Louis (Lonzo).

Nathaniel James, 3640 Marine avenue, St. Louis (Nathiell).

Ed Mills, 3640 Marine avenue, St. Louis.

Frederick Moser, 3110 Iowa avenue, St. Louis; 47 East Silver street, Butte, Mont. (Friederich, Fridrich).

William Smith, 1215 Gay street, St. Louis; State Penitentiary, Jefferson City, Mo.

Louis Turner, 3640 Marine avenue, St. Louis; 2346 Pine street, St. Louis.

Local Board for Division No. 11, City of St. Louis.

Walter Kendrick (Hendrick) Harris, 3933 S. Broadway, St. Louis.

Otto William Schmid, 3115 Utah street, St. Louis.

Wm. Harrison Walker, William Walker, 3825 Missouri avenue, St. Louis.

Jethro Worters, 2121 Gasconade street, St. Louis.

Local Board For Division No. 15, City of St. Louis.

Clyde Ames, 1900 California avenue, St. Louis.

William Davis, 2630 Papin street, St. Louis.

Fred Dial, 2008 Hickory street, St. Louis.

Jesse L. Dunnigan, 2637 Papin street, St. Louis. Jesse Dunnigan.

John Hearney, 2331 Hickory street, St. Louis.

Clyde Hendrichs (Hendricks), 2331 Papin street, St. Louis.

Raymond T. McDale (Thomas), 2701 Caroline street, St. Louis.

Robert R. Payton, 2621 Lafayette avenue, St. Louis; 1609 Oak street, Kansas City, Mo.

Ed Robertson, 1101 Ohio avenue, St. Louis.

Herman L. Rowald, 2022 Lafayette avenue, St. Louis; H. L., 2856 Euclid avenue, St. Louis.

Local Board for Division No. 18, City of St. Louis.

Edward Oren Black, Twenty-fifth and Montgomery, St. Louis.

Henry Kuehn, 2830 North Jefferson, St. Louis.

Wm. Reno, 2241A Dodier, St. Louis; W. Renn.

Thos. Stanton, 2233 Maiden Lane, St. Louis.

Local Board for Division No. 19, City of St. Louis.

Oregon Abington, 2933 Morgan street, St. Louis; Abbington.

Milton Barton, 2744 Morgan street, St. Louis.

Avoram B. Bendor, 2835 Dickson street, St. Louis; Averam B. Bender, Kirksville High School, Kirksville, Mo.; William B. Bender.

Jesse Bryant, 1003 Glasgow avenue, St. Louis.

Geo. Casey, 2709 Morgan street, St. Louis.

Sigmund Chernow, 3007 Dickson street, St. Louis.

Louis Engelhardt, 1722 Glasgow avenue, St. Louis.

Edw. Greshan, 3139 Bell avenue, St. Louis.

Erly B. Hollingsworth, 3936A Madison street, St. Louis; Earley B. Hollingworth.

Jas. Howard, 804 N. Leffingwell, St. Louis.

Wm. Johnson, 2830 Howard street, St. Louis.

Wm. Jones, 2933 Morgan street, St. Louis; 2833 Morgan street, St. Louis.

Jas. McFarland, 3704 Dickson street, St. Louis; James J. McFarland; James F. McFarland.

Wm. McGill, 2741 Morgan street, St. Louis.

Jno. Mewhaner, 920 North Leonard street, St. Louis.; John H. Newbauer, St. Louis.

Fillmore Mikel, 3126 Morgan street, St. Louis.

Jno. Murphy, 2801 Morgan street, St. Louis.

Geo. Perreu, 3033A Franklin avenue, St. Louis.

Joe Pierce, 2803 Morgan street, St. Louis.

Rob't C. Rechtene, 1716 Glasgow avenue, St. Louis; Rechtiene; Rechteine.

Jas. Jos. Robinson, 2939 Madison street, St. Louis; James J. Robinson, 2938 Madison, St. Louis.

Edgar Simmons, 2833 Lucas avenue, St. Louis; Edgar D. Simmons, 368 Adelaide, Toronto, Canada.

Hyman Zuckerman, 2840 Gamble street, St. Louis.

Local Board for Division No. 22, City of St. Louis.

L. Baker, 4237 Lucky street, St. Louis (Lorenze).

Broy Porter Gorum, 4055A Cook street, St. Louis (Troy).

Ed Haley, 4036 Evans avenue, St. Louis.

Roy Dee Hogg, 4831 St. Louis avenue, St. Louis (Roy De Hoog) (R. De Hoog).

Thos. McGarry, 4211WA Cook street, St. Louis.

Jno. J. McMurray, Valley Park, Mo. (2987A Abner place, St. Louis).

Walter M. Madison, 1220 N. Newstead street, St. Louis (Martin) (Madison).

Earl Pearson, 1308A N. Sarah street, St. Louis (Pierson).

Percival S. Robison, 4865 Cook avenue, St. Louis (P. S. Robson).

Ralph Smith, 4215W Kennerly street, St. Louis.

Geo. Thomas, 2629 Pendleton street, St. Louis (Thos.).

Local Board for Division No. 24, City of St. Louis.

Henry Bain, 4606 S. King's highway, St. Louis (Baine, 4600 S. King's highway, St. Louis) (Christy Clay Works, St. Louis).

Earl Bowles, 5563 Manchester, St. Louis (Boules).

Pietro Carelli, 1906 Cooper, St. Louis (Petro).

Michelo Fiele, 1225 Cooper avenue, St. Louis (Michelo).

John Edward Geiger, 5353 Reber place, St. Louis.

Earl Arnett Hall, 1024 Tamm avenue, St. Louis.

Arnett Earl Hall, 1104 Louisville avenue, St. Louis.

Tom Hunter, 4320 Hunt avenue, St. Louis.

John Jacobi, 5166 Eleanore, St. Louis (5264A Neosho street).

Charles Tony Link, 5927 Fyler avenue, St. Louis.

Bodine Neighbor, 6940 Manchester avenue, St. Louis.

William Osborne, 2703 Morganford road, St. Louis.

Ben Pointer, 4256 Norfolk avenue, St. Louis (Camp Doniphan, Ft. Sill, Ok.).

Wm. Lee Posey Jr., 4934 Lansdowne, St. Louis.

John Schmidt, 5937 Fyler avenue, St. Louis.

Richard E. Stone, 1567 Tower Grove avenue, St. Louis.

Troy Sullivan, 4320 Hunt avenue, St. Louis.

Edward Thayer, 4369 Vista avenue, St. Louis.

William Willis, 1331 Barran, St. Louis.

Local Board for Division No. 1, County of St. Louis.

Ernest Clark, Evans avenue, Clayton, Mo. (Earnest Clarke)

Jerry Curtis, 920 Hanly road, Clayton, Mo.

Horace Daniel, Evans avenue, Clayton, Mo. (Daniels)

Neal Evans, 6163 Gambleton place, St. Louis, Mo. (Ned).

Philip Fine, 908 Westgate, University City, Mo.

George Fleming, Webster Groves, Mo., Frankfort Heights, Ill.

William Flemming, Clayton, Mo. (William) (William Fleming).

Walter Gibson, Evans and Howard North and South roads, Clayton, Mo.

Wm. Arthur Greenhalgh, 464 West Lockwood, Webster Groves, Mo.; 3931 Pine, Philadelphia, Pa.

Edward B. Grogan, Washington University, University City, Mo. (Ed). Care of Y. M. C. A., Detroit, Mich.

Eugene Hamilton, Manchester road, Webster Groves, Mo.

Allen Hartfield, 84 Linden, Webster Groves, Mo. (Arthur Hartfield)

▲ Clarence Harrigan receiving his Selective Service notice, September 1917
Missouri Historical Society Collections
P0234-00038

➤ US military recruitment poster, ca. 1917
Library of Congress
LC-USZC4-9018

◄ Deserters and evaders list, ca. 1917
Missouri Historical Society Collections
A1771-00013

TRAINING AND SHIPPING OUT

St. Louisans from all walks of life answered the nation's call to arms, boarding trains in downtown St. Louis and at Jefferson Barracks that were headed for training camps across the country. For many it was their first time away from home; for some it was the last time they would ever see home.

Although St. Louisans served in every branch of the military, the majority were in the Army's 35th and 89th Infantry Divisions, which trained at Camp Funston in Kansas and Camp Doniphan in Oklahoma, respectively.

CAMP FUNSTON, KANSAS

"Let them whittle rifles out of wood." These were the orders Camp Funston's commander, Gen. Leonard Wood, gave upon hearing that the Fort Riley, Kansas–based camp didn't have enough equipment to begin training the 89th Infantry Division's newest recruits. The men, drawn largely from St. Louis and other parts of the Midwest, eventually received proper gear and trained for trench warfare from fall 1917 through spring 1918 before shipping overseas in June 1918.

Elements of the segregated 92nd Infantry Division and the 805th Pioneer Infantry Regiment also trained at Camp Funston. Two white soldiers had to be present at the camp for every one black soldier in each of these units, per an Army policy spurred by fears of arming African Americans and systemic racial prejudice in the military.

⌄ Camp Funston, located at Fort Riley, Kansas, October 1917
Library of Congress
2007664230

⌃ 89th Division soldiers exercising at Camp Funston, 1917
Missouri Historical Society Collections
P0229-01128

⌄ 89th Division soldiers learning how to set up a pup tent at Camp Funston, 1917
Missouri Historical Society Collections
P0229-01087

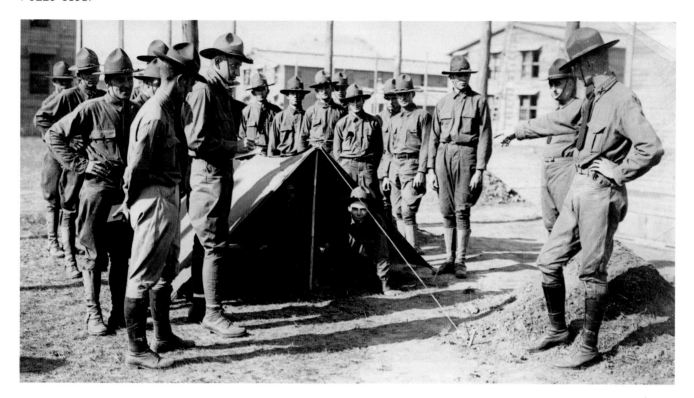

⌃ 89th Division soldiers playing baseball at Camp Funston, 1917
Missouri Historical Society Collections
P0229-01064

▲ **Southeast corner of Camp Doniphan, located at Fort Sill, Oklahoma, ca. 1917**
Soldiers Memorial Military Museum Collections
SMX03667

CAMP DONIPHAN, OKLAHOMA

"Camp Doniphan, from a soldier's point of view, lacked everything but dust. . . . The [camp] routed the soldiers out of bed each morning with dust in their eyes and dust on their army bacon."

Such was the fate of members of the Missouri and Kansas National Guard and volunteers, including the newly recruited 5th Missouri Infantry Regiment, who began their formal Army training at Camp Doniphan in Fort Sill, Oklahoma. Between September 1917 and April 1918 they learned how to fight in trenches with bayonets, hand grenades, and gas masks.

The National Guardsmen were also reorganized into the Army's 35th Infantry Division, which included more than 14,500 Missourians out of a total of 27,000 men. Most of the St. Louisans served in the division's 138th Infantry Regiment and 128th Field Artillery. Numerous National Guard officers were dismissed as part of the reorganization—a leadership change that proved disastrous when the 35th Division went into combat during the Meuse-Argonne Offensive.

▲ **35th Division soldiers at Camp Doniphan, ca. 1917**
Missouri Historical Society Collections
P0484-00018

⌃ **Training trenches at Camp Doniphan, ca. 1917**
Courtesy of the National World War I Museum and Memorial,
Kansas City, Missouri, U.S.A.
1980.48.14

⌃ 35th Division soldiers standing at attention at Camp Doniphan, ca. 1917
Missouri Historical Society Collections
P0484-00006

➤ 35th Division soldiers exercising at Camp Doniphan, ca. 1917
Missouri Historical Society Collections
P0484-00019

◄ 5th Missouri Infantry Regiment recruitment poster, ca. 1917
Missouri Historical Society Collections
N21939

U. S. NAVY

Courtesy of Life

Drawn by Charles Dana Gibson

"Here he is, Sir."
We need him and you too!
Navy Recruiting Station

➤ **Great Lakes Naval Training Station, ca. 1917**
Missouri Historical Society Collections
P0157-19193

GREAT LAKES NAVAL TRAINING STATION, ILLINOIS

St. Louisans joined the US Navy expecting to serve in Europe and across the world. Instead, most newly drafted and volunteer sailors spent the war at the Great Lakes Naval Training Station in Illinois. Many did, however, play a large role in demobilization efforts after the war, transporting nearly 2 million Americans home from overseas.

Second only to the Army in enlistment during World War I, the Navy was no match for its European foes—or its allies. In the years leading up to the war, Great Britain and Germany had been in a naval arms race while the United States had focused on isolationism, resulting in a diminished US Navy. America set about producing new warships after entering the war, but those were many months in the making. In the meantime, the US Navy focused on transporting troops and supplies to Europe, as well as training Navy officers and seamen for the forthcoming warships.

➤ **US Navy recruitment ad, ca. 1918**
Missouri Historical Society Collections
A1771-00001

◀ **US Navy recruitment poster, 1917**
Library of Congress
LC-USZC4-10240

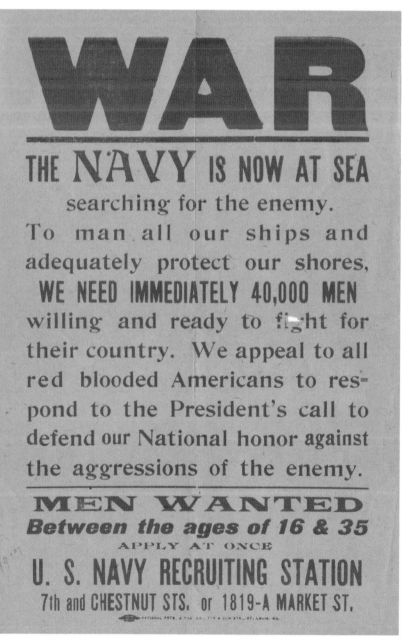

▼ **Aviation students lined up at Scott Field on inspection day, ca. 1918**
Missouri Historical Society Collections
P0015-00006

ST. LOUIS POST-DISPATCH — TUESDAY EVENING, SEPTEMBER 18, 1917. — ST. LOUIS POST-DISPATCH

Aviation Students at Scott Field Lined Up Before a Curtiss Biplane on Inspection Day

Left to right, lower row: J. F. Wehner, M. C. White, B. B. Bird, R. F. Potter, L. G. Meister, W. A. Thomson, M. D. Friedman, W. D. Grant, C. J. Cleary and C. E. Pyle.
Middle row: A. M. Kidder, N. E. Pierson, R. M. Phelps, H. H. McVey, F. G. Ragsdale, L. G. Woodward, W. T. Martin and R. T. Robinson.
Upper row: I. D. Stone, J. H. Maupin, R. E. Ellis, J. T. Luhr, T. E. Alexander, J. U. Wegener, J. T. McAteer, T. C. Rockstroh, S. T. Webster, H. M. Pierce, J. R. McClushion and B. C. J. Somers.

SCOTT FIELD, ILLINOIS

With entry into the war came the need to increase the number of military pilots—and aviation fields at which to train them. Hoping to secure one of these fields in the region, aviation proponent Albert Bond Lambert, the St. Louis Chamber of Commerce, and the Greater Belleville Board of Trade negotiated for 624 acres of land near Belleville, Illinois, on which Scott Field could be built. Construction began in June 1917 and was completed two months later.

Named for Cpl. Frank Scott, the first US enlisted man killed in an aviation crash, Scott Field trained pilots in mapmaking, enemy spotting, and dogfighting. By the end of the war, more than 300 pilots and ground crew had trained at the site now known as Scott Air Force Base.

∧ Scott Field, ca. 1918
Greater St. Louis Air and Space Museum,
Gerald Balzer Collection

CAMP GAILLARD, MISSOURI

Moving supplies and troops across Europe required the creation of an effective railroad infrastructure. Recruited largely from St. Louis railroad men and engineers, the 12th Engineers laid miles of railroad in France.

They began training in June 1917 at Camp Gaillard, located near the present-day Chain of Rocks Bridge. Living on barges moored on the Mississippi River, the men practiced building, repairing, and maintaining rail lines. Two months later, the 12th Engineers became some of the first American troops sent overseas.

⌄ Engineers Club of St. Louis presenting flag to 12th Engineers at Camp Gaillard, July 1917
Missouri Historical Society Collections
P0015-00021

⌃ Company E, 12th Engineers at Camp Gaillard, 1917
Soldiers Memorial Military Museum Collections
SMX03675

ST. LOUISANS OVER THERE

The first St. Louisans arrived in Europe in June 1917. By the end of the war they were spread across France, serving as soldiers, doctors, nurses, singers, cooks, railroad men, and engineers.

From the first Chief Nurse of the Army, Maj. Julia Stimson, to Medal of Honor recipients Cpt. Alexander Skinker and Sgt. Michael Ellis, St. Louisans served with distinction and courage, and they contributed mightily to the war effort overseas.

They also witnessed firsthand how World War I forever changed the nature of combat. Chemical and trench warfare, airplanes, machine guns, and tanks all made their deadly debuts during the Great War, leading to a staggering total of 8.2 million combat deaths.

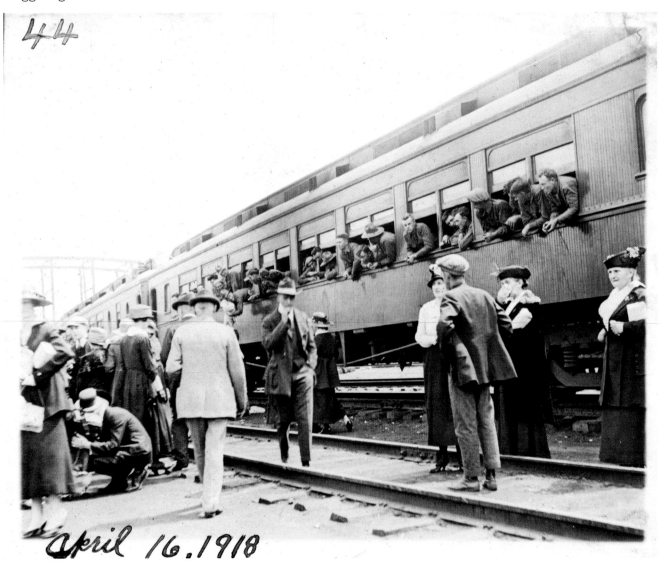

89TH INFANTRY DIVISION

The days of training with wooden rifles on the Kansas plains were long behind the 27,000 men of the 89th Infantry Division when they arrived in France in June 1918. They reached the front lines that August and saw nearly continuous action for the next three months, during which they played an integral role in the success of the St. Mihiel Offensive and the decisive Meuse-Argonne Offensive.

▲ **138th Infantry Regiment aboard troop train bound for the East Coast, ca. 1918**
Missouri Historical Society Collections
P0821-01-044

➤ **Map showing the 89th Division sector in the St. Mihiel Offensive, 1918**
Soldiers Memorial Military Museum Collections
SMX00283

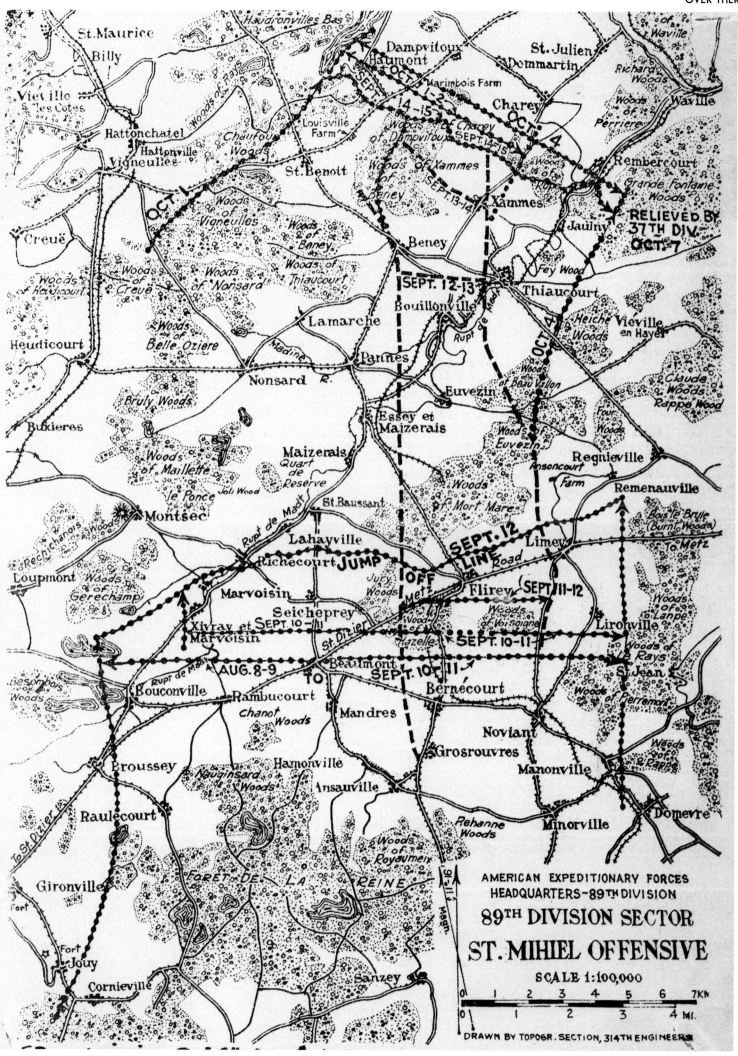

AMERICAN EXPEDITIONARY FORCES
HEADQUARTERS~89TH DIVISION
89TH DIVISION SECTOR
ST. MIHIEL OFFENSIVE
SCALE 1:100,000

DRAWN BY TOPOGR. SECTION, 314TH ENGINEERS

> Map showing the 89th Division sector in the Meuse-Argonne Offensive, 1918
Soldiers Memorial Military Museum Collections
SMX00284

‹ 89th Division uniform patch, ca. 1917
Missouri Historical Society Collections
2010-029-0022

˅ 89th Division resting, ca. 1918
Missouri Historical Society Collections
P0157-002-19229

˅ Gen. Pershing decorating officers of the 89th Division, ca. 1918
Missouri Historical Society Collections
P0157-V19230

V19229 Doughboys of 89th Div., Resting Before Review, Treves, Germany.

V19230 General Pershing Decorating Officers of 89th Div., Treves, Germany.

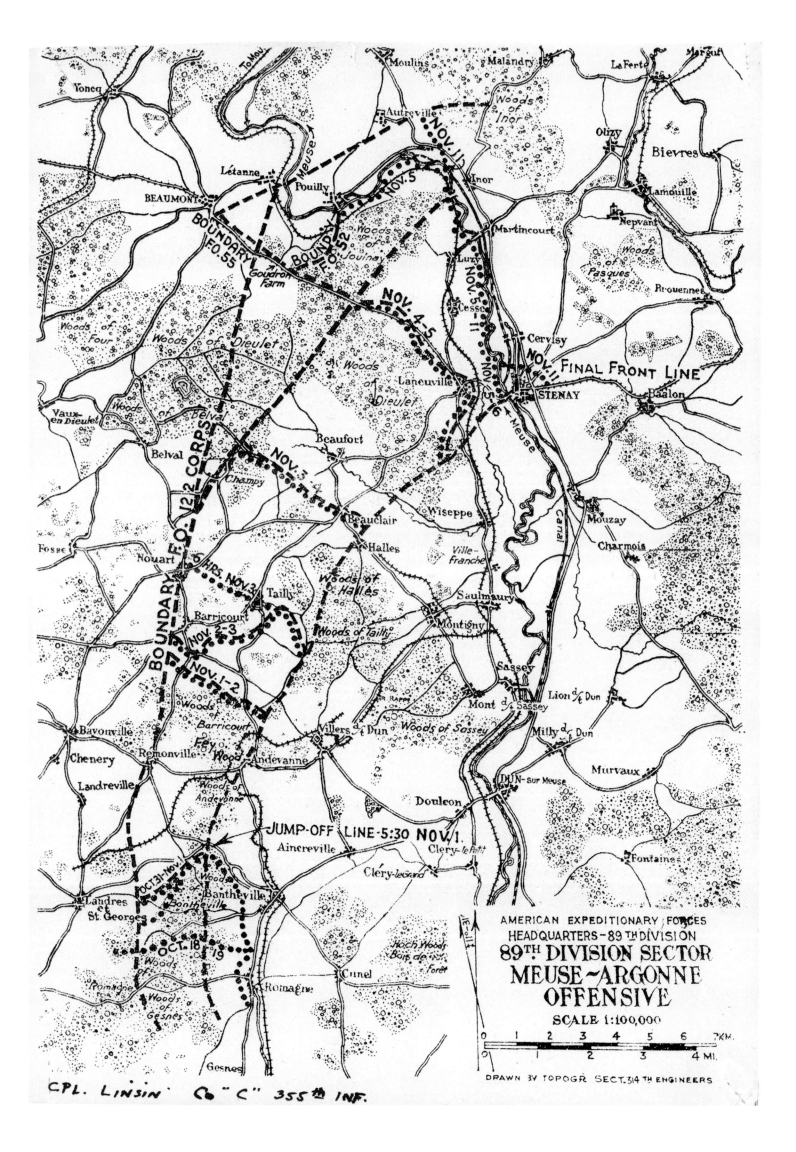

AMERICAN EXPEDITIONARY FORCES
HEADQUARTERS - 89TH DIVISION
89TH DIVISION SECTOR
MEUSE~ARGONNE
OFFENSIVE

SCALE 1:100,000

DRAWN BY TOPOGR SECT. 314TH ENGINEERS

CPL. LINSIN Co "C" 355TH INF.

◄ **Sgt. Arthur Forrest, ca. 1918**
Soldiers Memorial Military Museum Collections
SMX00125

SERGEANT ARTHUR FORREST, COMPANY D, 354TH INFANTRY, 89TH DIVISION

Professional baseball player Arthur Forrest enlisted in the US Army in 1917 and arrived in France on June 4, 1918, as part of the 89th Infantry Division. He quickly formed bonds with his fellow soldiers on the battlefield much as he did with his baseball teammates back home.

Sgt. Forrest's commitment to his comrades was best represented when his company was halted in the small French town of Rémonville by a hail of fire from a nest of six enemy machine guns. To save his comrades, Forrest single-handedly crawled to within 50 yards of the nest and then charged, catching the enemy by surprise and driving them from the area. For his actions, Forrest received the Medal of Honor, the nation's greatest military award.

➤ **Map of the 35th Division's movements during the Meuse-Argonne Offensive, 1918**
Missouri Historical Society Collections
A1771-00020

⌃ **German MG-08/15 machine gun of the type faced by Sgt. Arthur Forrest, ca. 1917**
Soldiers Memorial Military Museum Collections
SM2015-000-0331

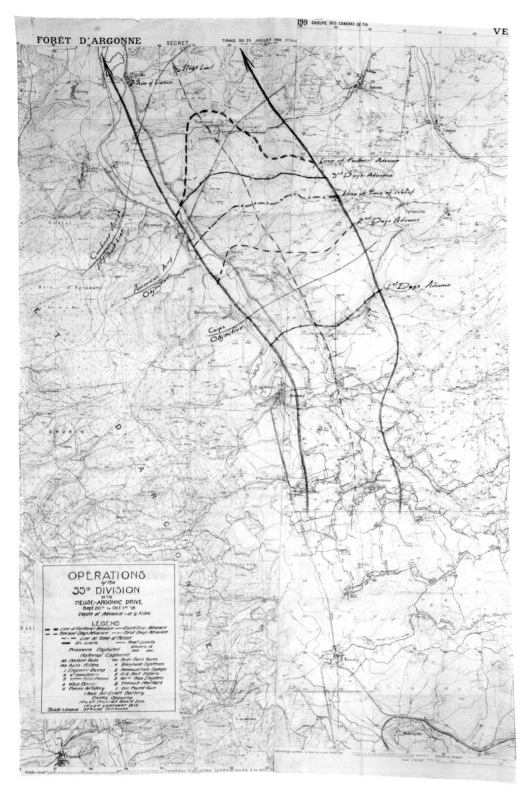

THE 35TH INFANTRY DIVISION AND ITS COLLAPSE AT MEUSE-ARGONNE

The 35th Infantry Division arrived at the front lines in the Vosges Mountains in June 1918 and remained there, training, until September 1918. The months of training culminated in the division's first major assignment: forming the left flank of the Meuse-Argonne Offensive, the largest in US military history.

On September 26, 1918, the lead units of the 35th Division began advancing toward heavily fortified German positions. From the start, communication and leadership breakdowns plagued the troops. St. Louis's 138th Infantry Regiment led the attack but suffered under constant fire and failed to achieve its objectives. By October 1, five days after the offensive began, more than 20,000 Kansans and Missourians were sent back from the front and saw only limited action for the remainder of the war.

Despite this outcome, numerous members of the 35th Division, including many St. Louisans, distinguished themselves overseas—one was a future US president from Missouri.

77-4

CAPTAIN HARRY S. TRUMAN, BATTERY D, 129TH FIELD ARTILLERY, 35TH DIVISION

Among the Missouri National Guarden called on to serve was future president and Missouri native Harry Truman. Rejected by West Point for having poor eyesight, Truman served in the Missouri National Guard to fulfill his military aspirations.

When the Missouri National Guard became the 35th Infantry Division of the US Army during the war, Truman rose to the rank of captain. He commanded Battery D of the 129th Field Artillery at Vosges, St. Mihiel, Meuse-Argonne, and Verdun.

Today the 129th Field Artillery operates as part of the Missouri National Guard under the nickname Truman's Own.

◄ Cpt. Harry Truman, ca. 1918
Courtesy Harry S. Truman Presidential Library
77-4

CORPORAL GEORGE VONLAND, COMPANY H, 138TH INFANTRY, 35TH DIVISION

St. Louisan George Vonland enlisted with the Missouri National Guard in 1916 and went on to serve with Company H in the 138th Infantry Regiment of the 35th Infantry Division. While in the Vosges Mountains, Cpl. Vonland was part of a raid near Hilsenfirst, France. His heroic actions during this raid, which he recalled in a journal of his experiences titled *My Days in France,* earned him the Distinguished Service Cross and the French Croix de Guerre.

Vonland was later promoted to sergeant and fought in the Meuse-Argonne Offensive, during which he was wounded.

➤ Cpl. George Vonland, 1918
Missouri Historical Society Collections
P0649-00011

CAPTAIN ALEXANDER SKINKER, COMPANY I, 138TH INFANTRY, 35TH DIVISION

"He died, as he had lived, protecting his men."
—Col. Edmund J. McMahon, former commander of the 138th Infantry Regiment

Alexander Skinker was the son of prominent St. Louis lawyer Thomas Skinker, who built the first electric railway in St. Louis County. After graduating from Washington University in St. Louis in 1905, Alexander Skinker spent several years as an officer in the Missouri National Guard.

On September 26, 1918, Cpt. Skinker and his men found themselves on the leading edge of the largest offensive in US history. Alongside St. Louisans he had served with for years, Skinker advanced toward German positions—and was immediately halted by intense machine-gun fire. To make the advance safe for the rest of his unit, Skinker and two others bravely assaulted the German position. Within moments they were struck down by German fire.

For sacrificing his life so his men might live, Cpt. Skinker received the Medal of Honor. More than 5,000 people attended his burial in Bellefontaine Cemetery, a testament to the great respect with which he was regarded by the entire St. Louis community.

THE 92ND AND 93RD INFANTRY DIVISIONS

"I commend the 92nd Division for its achievements not only in the field, but on the record its men have made in their individual conduct. The American public has every reason to be proud of the record made by the 92nd Division."—Gen. John Pershing, review of the 92nd Division, January 28, 1919

Prior to the arrival of the African American 92nd and 93rd Infantry Divisions in France in the summer of 1918, political uproar raged in the still-segregated United States about arming black soldiers. Gen. Pershing responded by assigning these combat troops to the French army. Wearing US uniforms and armed with French equipment, the men of the 93rd Division distinguished themselves in French service, ultimately adopting the French combat helmet as their insignia.

The soldiers of the 92nd Division trained under the French when they arrived overseas, but unlike the 93rd, they served under American command at the end of the war. The 92nd Division was on the front lines in the final days of the Meuse-Argonne Offensive and greatly impressed Gen. Pershing, who oversaw the entire American Army.

⌃ **French Adrian helmet of the type worn by African American troops attached to the French army, ca. 1917**
Soldiers Memorial Military Museum Collections
SM1997-018-0028

ʌ French Fusil semiautomatic rifle, model 1917, ca. 1917
Soldiers Memorial Military Museum Collections
SMX00420

ᵛ 369th Infantry soldiers serving in French trenches, ca. 1918
Photographs and Prints Division, Schomburg Center for Research in Black Culture, The New York Public Library, Astor, Lenox and Tilden Foundations
4034617

> 117th Field Signal Battalion operating telephone switchboard in Essey, Meurthe-et-Moselle, France, September 1918
Courtesy of the National World War I Museum and Memorial, Kansas City, Missouri, U.S.A.
1981.74.38

THE 42ND INFANTRY DIVISION

The 42nd Infantry Division was raised from draftees and National Guardsmen from 26 states and Washington, DC. Missourians, including St. Louisans, were among those represented, with elements of the Missouri National Guard forming the division's 117th Field Signal Battalion. During training, Col. Douglas MacArthur commented that "the 42nd Division stretches like a rainbow from one end of America to the other."

⌄ **12th Engineers marching through London, 1917**
Soldiers Memorial Military Museum Collections
SMX03534-005

THE 12TH ENGINEERS OF ST. LOUIS OVERSEAS

One of the earliest American units to arrive overseas, the 12th Engineers of St. Louis reached England in August 1917. While there, they headed a parade of American troops in London, marking the first time since William the Conqueror in 1066 that an armed foreign army had marched along the city's streets. The parade was hailed in the press as a showing of momentous Anglo-American relations.

In August 1917 the 12th Engineers were assigned to operate behind the British front, building and maintaining rail lines. In July 1918 the men were reassigned to the US Army and supported operations through the end of the war in November 1918.

The construction, maintenance, and operation of railroads provided swift, strategic movement of matériel and troops over long distances, allowing the Allies to strike the Germans where they were weakest along the front. This capability proved essential to the Allies' success during the Meuse-Argonne Offensive.

› **12th Engineers camp at Ménil-la-Tour, France, 1918**
Missouri Historical Society Collections
P0389-046437

⌄ 12th Engineers next to locomotive in Belleville, France, 1918
Missouri Historical Society Collections
P0389-000019

> **USS *Leviathan* transport ship, ca. 1918**
Naval History and Heritage Command
NH 71

⌄ **Great Lakes Naval Training Station, ca. 1917**
Missouri Historical Society Collections
P0157-19193

19193   Thousands of Uncle Sam's Sailors, Training
Station, Great Lakes, Ill.

MISSOURI'S "DRY LAND SAILORS"

More than 14,000 Missourians enlisted in the US Navy, making it the military branch with the second largest number of Missouri members, after the US Army. Because the Navy's role during the war largely consisted of transporting troops and supplies, as well as conducting submarine patrols in the Atlantic and Mediterranean, most Missourians in the Navy remained at US-based training stations as "dry land sailors." These men didn't sail the ocean until after the war ended, when they transported troops back from Europe, primarily through the French port of Brest.

> **Aerial view of harbor and city of Brest, France, ca. 1918**
Naval History and Heritage Command
NH 2337

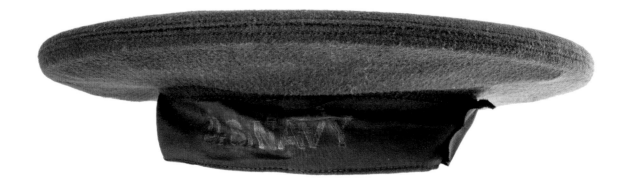

‹ ⌃ **US Navy uniform and cap of SF Frank Mitchell, ca. 1918**
Missouri Historical Society Collections
2005-079-0001a, 2005-079-0001b, 2005-079-0001c,
2005-079-0001d

› **Apron made of Navy neckerchief and hat band given to Edna Kessler by SF Frank Mitchell, ca. 1918**
Missouri Historical Society Collections
2005-079-0019

SHIPFITTER FRANK MITCHELL, US NAVY

"Well dear this sure is a great life the only thing a fellow don't have a lot of time for his self we have had our navy drill changed to the army drill so I guess they are getting us ready for the trenches but I sure like the army drill better for it don't wear our shoes out so quick and it is easy on the feet."—SF Frank Mitchell to Edna Kessler, August 25, 1918

Frank Mitchell was among the many St. Louisans who spent the war at Great Lakes Naval Training Station in Illinois. While there, SF Mitchell often wrote to his sweetheart and future wife, Edna Kessler.

His dissatisfaction with Navy life was clear in his occasional signature of "Same old dry land sailor" and comments like, "I seen more of a ship in St. Louis than I will ever see at the Great Lakes."

Mitchell finally made it onto a ship in the summer of 1919. He was assigned to the USS *El Sol*, a freighter that carried American troops back from Europe during demobilization. Mitchell made two transatlantic trips on the ship before he was discharged.

> **SF Frank Mitchell, ca. 1918**
Missouri Historical Society Collections
P0942-00001

‹ USS *El Sol*, 1919
Naval History and Heritage Command
NH 102941

› US Marines recruitment poster featuring German nickname for Devil Dogs, 1917
Library of Congress
LC-USZC4-10224

⌄ Ship's officers and crew of the USS *El Sol*, February 1919
Naval History and Heritage Command
NH 103099

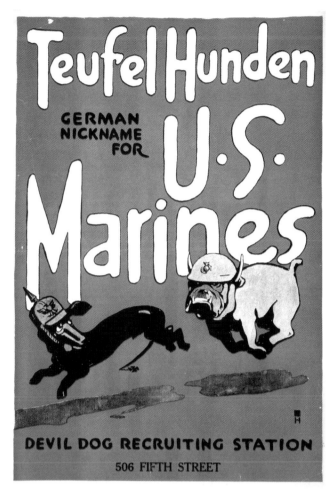

> **US Marines recruitment ad, ca. 1918**
Missouri Historical Society Collections
A1771-00002

THE MARINE CORPS, 4TH AND 5TH MARINE BRIGADES

During the war the Marine Corps grew to 75,000 strong, including 3,721 Missourians. Though small in number compared to the other branches, the Marine Corps became internationally famous for its toughness and fierce fighting, earning the nickname "Devil Dogs."

The Marines saw especially intense fighting in 1918 during the Battle of Belleau Wood and the Meuse-Argonne Offensive. At Belleau Wood, Marine gunnery sergeant Fred Stockham gave his gas mask to St. Louisan Barak Mattingly, an act that saved Mattingly's life and posthumously earned Stockham the Medal of Honor and a St. Louis American Legion Post namesake.

> **US Marines in Belleau Wood, ca. 1918**
Courtesy of the National World War I Museum and Memorial, Kansas City, Missouri, U.S.A.
1989.24.33

PROCLAMATION!

CITIZENS OF ST. LOUIS:

YOU ARE GOING TO ENLIST!

Deep rooted in your intensely American hearts is the conviction that you will bear arms in the defense of our beloved country.

You will offer your services today—tomorrow at the latest—in some branch of the national defense.

But which branch—that's the question!

To the person inexperienced in military affairs, the question immediately arises—in which branch of the service shall I enlist?

Will the active service be on land or sea?

Did you ever hear of the UNITED STATES MARINE CORPS?

It operates on both land and sea.

Wherever there's fighting—be it on land or sea or in the air, you'll find Marines in the thick of it.

Marines dress like soldiers although they are trained in some of the duties of sailors. On shipboard they man the torpedo defense batteries.

Red-blooded men looking for action should find plenty of it with the soldiers of the sea.

Marines have shown the way to our fighting men since 1798 and they are always "first in" when the war bugles blow.

The Marine Corps maintains separate recruiting stations and you cannot enlist in this important branch of the national defense other than at a Marine Corps recruiting station.

The Marine Corps recruiting station in St. Louis is at 215 Fullerton Building.

In making choice of service don't forget the Marines!

It is a sort of super-service.

George Barnett

AVIATION SECTION, ARMY SIGNAL CORPS

St. Louis has always been a city of flight, and World War I was no exception. From Maj. Albert Bond Lambert's work with Army balloonists in south St. Louis to the hundreds of pilots and ground crew trained at the newly built Scott Field, St. Louis contributed mightily to the aviation aspect of the war effort.

The use of aircraft on the battlefield was both groundbreaking and dangerous. As the war progressed, specialized classes of aircraft emerged, including fighters and bombers that battled in the skies over the trenches.

MAJOR ALBERT BOND LAMBERT, ARMY SIGNAL CORPS

St. Louis native Albert Bond Lambert, a major in the Army Signal Corps, worked with the Missouri Aeronautical Society to establish a training camp for balloon pilots at the intersection of S. Grand Blvd. and Meramec St. in south St. Louis. Balloonists were trained to pilot balloons, make maps, and provide signals to troops on the ground. Maj. Lambert later oversaw a larger training base at Camp John Wise near San Antonio, Texas. After the war, he worked to bring St. Louis an airport that now bears his name.

‹ Lt. Albert Bond Lambert, ca. 1917
St. Louis Post-Dispatch

THE COURSE OF WORLD WAR I

Shortly after the war's start in 1914, momentum slowed, and no significant ground was gained or lost by either side for the next three years. In 1918, with fears of what a surge of US troops might bring, Germany launched a spring offensive in an attempt to win the war before American reinforcements could arrive. The Allies blocked the German maneuver and cleared the way for the summertime arrival of American soldiers who poured into Europe, bringing with them a renewed sense of hope—and the beginning of the end of the war.

▲ **French M1915 Chauchat light machine gun, ca. 1917**
Soldiers Memorial Military Museum Collections
SM1938-020-0002_0001

▲ **US M1903 Springfield rifle, ca. 1918**
Missouri Historical Society Collections
1981-003-0077

▲ **US M1917 Enfield rifle, ca. 1918**
Missouri Historical Society Collections
1981-003-0078

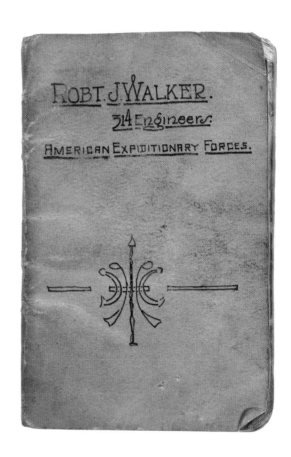

▲ **Prayer book of Sgt. Robert Walker, ca. 1918**
Missouri Historical Society Collections
2010-029-0010

◄ **Transportation Corps uniform of Pvt. William Eydmann, ca. 1917**
Missouri Historical Society Collections
2008-143-0001

▾ **German MG 08/15 machine gun, ca. 1917**
Soldiers Memorial Military Museum Collections
SMX00320

▴ **German Stahlhelm helmet, model 1916, ca. 1917**
Soldiers Memorial Military Museum Collections
SM1938-001-0001

▼ **German hand grenade, model 17, ca. 1917**
Soldiers Memorial Military Museum Collections
SMX00538

▼ **German wound badge collected by Cpt. John Hardesty, ca. 1917**
Missouri Historical Society Collections
2006-092-0030

▲ **German Gewehr 98 rifle, ca. 1917**
Soldiers Memorial Military Museum Collections
SM1941-007-0043

◄ ∨ **German Iron Cross medal collected by Cpl. Irving Muhs at St. Mihiel, ca. 1917**
Missouri Historical Society Collections
1926-044-0001

◄ ▼ German Pickelhaube helmet, ca. 1917
Soldiers Memorial Military Museum Collections
SM1939-024-0001

The longevity of the war combined with naval blockades led to shortages of materials and food across Germany. In response, many substitute or "ersatz" materials were used, including paper-cloth, coffee made from roasted acorns and nuts, and wood-soled canvas shoes.

➤ **Newspaper clipping titled "Edible Earth New Food Substitute in Germany," ca. 1918**
Missouri Historical Society Collections
A0258-00001

◄ **Identification tag of German soldier Karl Diem collected by Cpl. Irving Muhs at St. Mihiel, ca. 1917**
Missouri Historical Society Collections
1926-044-0005

⌄ **German wood-soled canvas military boots, ca. 1918**
Missouri Historical Society Collections
1919-00-0008

EDIBLE EARTH NEW FOOD SUBSTITUTE IN GERMANY

Learned Professors Tell People It Was Esteemed a Delicacy During 30 Years' War.

AMSTERDAM, Dec. 14.—In their frantic search for new food substitutes Germans have made the discovery that so-called edible earth exists in many parts of Germany, and learned professors have lost no time in making it known that the eating of earth is by no means confined to certain savage tribes of New Guinea and South America.

It was a highly esteemed delicacy, they say, during the 30 Years' War, and also in the "lean years" between 1719 and 1733.

Layers of edible earth, it is stated, have been located on the moors of Luneburg, near Koenigsberg, in the valley of the lower Vistula and in the Grand Duchy of Hesse, while the Austrians, it is announced, have their own deposits of edible earth near Eger and Franzensbad, in Bohemia.

TRENCH WARFARE

"As soon as we get out of our trench we are met with a murderous machine-gun fire. Walker and Melton killed, Barbee and McLoney wounded. A shower of 'iron apples' [grenades] silenced the machine-gun. Shell lands close, knocked down but not hurt. Schultze hit in the arm, a piece of shrapnel goes through Kolms both jaws. Our artillery tore up the bosche [German] wire in good shape, and we expierenced little trouble in getting through. We hit their front line to-gether, it seemed as if every man had gotten their at the same time."—Cpl. George Vonland, 138th Infantry, 35th Division, from *My Days in France,* July 6, 1918

Synonymous with World War I, opposing trench systems stretched hundreds of miles from the Swiss Alps to the North Sea. St. Louisans were among the soldiers who ate, slept, laughed, and fought for their lives in these trenches.

The space between trenches was No Man's Land, a desolate, cratered wasteland that remained virtually unchanged for four years. Soldiers eventually charged across No Man's Land, braving whizzing bullets and deafening explosions, to bring an end to the bloody stalemate.

⌃ **117th Field Signal Battalion laying telephone wire into frontline trenches near Manonviller, France, March 1918**
Courtesy of the National World War I Museum and Memorial, Kansas City, Missouri, U.S.A.
1926.28.32

⌃ **Two American soldiers peering over a trench, ca. 1918**
Soldiers Memorial Military Museum Collections
SMX02554-062

➤ **German "Lobster" body armor, ca. 1917**
Soldiers Memorial Military Museum Collections
SM1940-076-0007

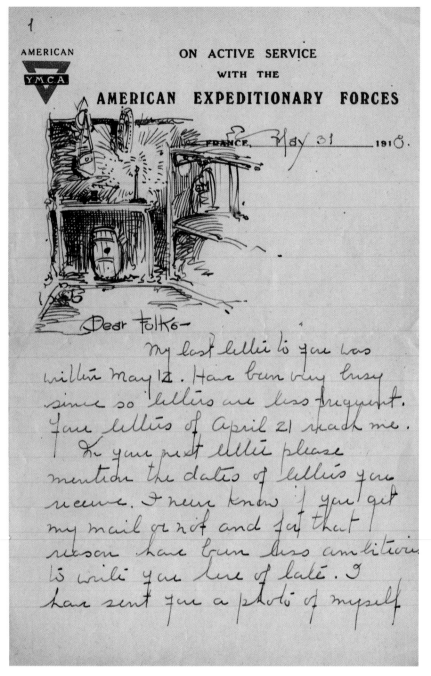

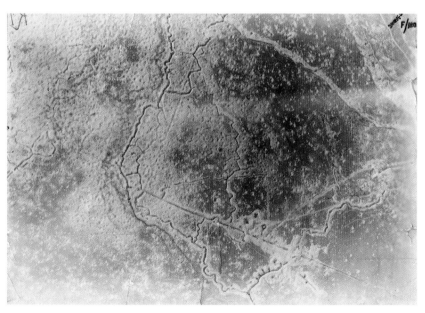

> Trench periscope and case of Pvt. Harry Russell, ca. 1918
Soldiers Memorial Military Museum Collections
SM1940-106-0001

< Trench "dugout" sketch by Cpl. George Maguolo, 29th Engineers, ca. 1918
Missouri Historical Society Collections
A0969-00004_0001

< View of trenches at the Hilsenfirst summit in the Vosges Mountains, ca. 1918
Soldiers Memorial Military Museum Collections
SMX03831

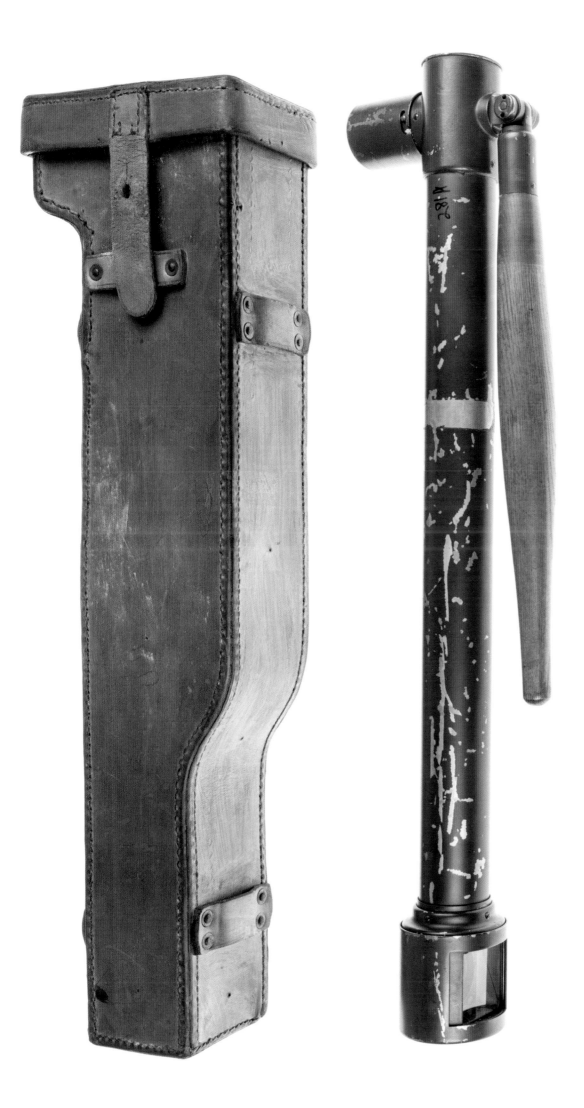

COMMUNICATIONS: FROM PIGEON TO PHONE

World War I saw a blend of old and new communication methods. Although military leaders were learning and adapting to the often undependable instant telecommunications, they still relied on hand-carried messages and carrier pigeons to deliver orders. At the same time, communications from aerial observers provided an unprecedented perspective of the battlefield.

The Missourians of the 117th Field Signal Battalion were among the telecommunications units running and maintaining wires to connect commanders to their troops in the field.

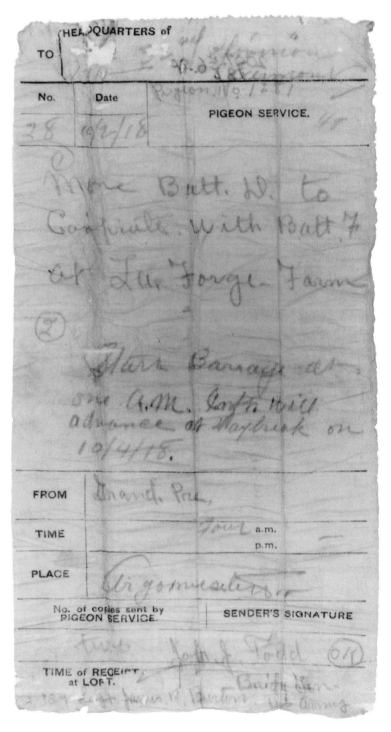

˄ German field telephone and case, ca. 1918
Missouri Historical Society Collections
1925-044-0001

˂ Two soldiers preparing a message for a carrier pigeon to transport, ca. 1918
Courtesy of the National World War I Museum and Memorial, Kansas City, Missouri, U.S.A.
1986.19.4.51

˄ Carrier pigeon capsule and message, 1918
Missouri Historical Society Collections
2007-056-0018

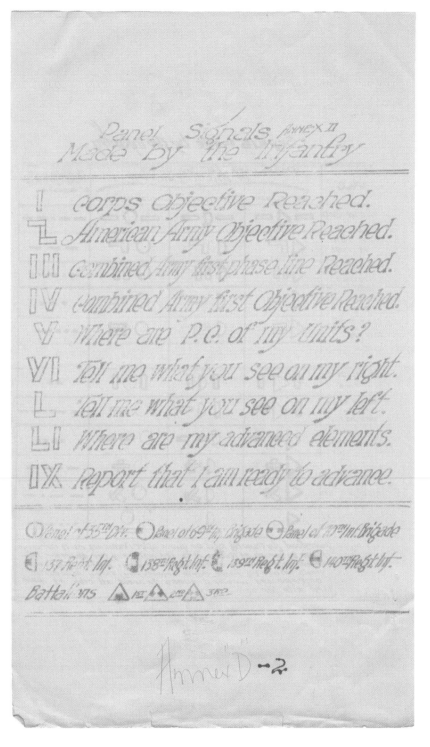

➤ 117th Field Signal Battalion operating field radio set in Baccarat, France, May 1918
Courtesy of the National World War I Museum and Memorial, Kansas City, Missouri, U.S.A.
1981.74.28

◀ ⌄ Guide to signaling aircraft, with instructions, ca. 1918
Missouri Historical Society Collections
A1771-00017

➤ Interior of 117th Field Signal Battalion telephone exchange in Brouville, France, April 1918
Courtesy of the National World War I Museum and Memorial, Kansas City, Missouri, U.S.A.
1981.74.22

GAS WARFARE

Choking, burning, blistering, blindness, and death—all were effects of the deadly gas deployed across Europe during World War I. Chemical warfare first took the form of tear gas in 1914, but efforts to break the stalemate led to the development of the more lethal mustard and chlorine gases that were used extensively by both sides through the war's end.

Many St. Louisans were forever scarred by gas attacks, sometimes succumbing to their injuries later in life. Attempts were made to combat this silent killer, including gas masks of varying effectiveness and all manner of warning devices to notify soldiers of gas attacks.

⌃ **US Corrected English (CE) model gas mask, ca. 1917**
Soldiers Memorial Military Museum Collections
SMX03218

➤ **American soldiers training on how to use gas masks, ca. 1918**
Missouri Historical Society Collections
P0157-013-19198

▲ **Gas-attack warning bell next to American field ambulance, ca. 1917**
Library of Congress
LC-DIG-ggbain-23114

◄ **German G-17 Lederschützmaske gas mask and carrier, ca. 1918**
Missouri Historical Society Collections
X00113

CIVILIAN WAR WORKERS

St. Louis civilians were instrumental in keeping American troops in fighting form. From Red Cross ambulance drivers and nurses providing medical care to Salvation Army and YMCA hut workers dishing up food and entertainment, privately funded organizations played a significant role in the war.

‹ **YMCA fundraising poster, 1918**
Missouri Historical Society Collections
P0299-00142

WILLIAM DANFORTH, YMCA

Without the war, one of St. Louis's most famous products wouldn't have its name. William Danforth, founder of St. Louis–based Ralston-Purina, never shied away from a challenge, so it's no surprise that he joined the YMCA at age 47 as a way to aid America's war effort. Danforth's assignment in 1918 was to establish canteens and recreation centers for the more than 27,000 men of the 3rd Infantry Division. While serving these troops, Danforth first heard the term used universally by American soldiers to describe food: "chow." After Danforth returned home, he trademarked the term "chow," substituted it for "feed" on all of his company's products, and Purina Chow was born.

▲ **Charles Atkinson Bull, ca. 1918**
Missouri Historical Society Collections
P0649-00012

CHARLES ATKINSON BULL, YMCA

On March 17, 1918, Charles Atkinson Bull, a well-known St. Louis gospel singer, religious worker, and piano salesman, departed for France. Carrying with him this portable Estey pump organ, Bull joined the 25,925 YMCA volunteers serving overseas and in America. The YMCA provided entertainment, support, and religious services to US and Allied troops during World War I.

‹ **YMCA secretary William Danforth distributing cigars to 3rd Infantry Division soldiers, ca. 1918**
Missouri Historical Society Collections
GRA00180

**◄ ▲ Portable Estey pump organ used by Charles
Atkinson Bull with the YMCA, 1892**
Missouri Historical Society Collections
1987-086-0001

ST. LOUIS MEDICINE: BASE HOSPITAL 21

Not all battles happened on the front line. The St. Louisans of Base Hospital 21 fought the war with scalpels, X-rays, and medicine.

Located behind British lines on a racetrack in Rouen, France, the staff of Base Hospital 21 consisted of 28 officers, 65 nurses, and 185 enlisted men drawn from the faculty and students of Washington University in St. Louis. A typical day saw a turnover of nearly 100 patients, which skyrocketed to more than 500 per day during heavy fighting. Over the course of 18 strenuous months, St. Louis doctors and nurses treated more than 60,000 patients.

Base Hospital 21 was a leader in the use of X-rays to aid surgery. It used more X-ray plates than all other base hospitals in France combined. The hospital also served as the region's center for neurological disorders, often treating upward of 300 cases of "war neurosis" at one time. The hospital's staff won wide recognition, including the promotion of several of its doctors and its chief nurse to prominent positions during the war.

WAR NEUROSIS

"Shell shock" and "war neurosis" were terms used during World War I to describe a variety of symptoms better understood today as PTSD, or post-traumatic stress disorder. These symptoms included hypersensitivity, tinnitus, amnesia, headaches, and tremors. PTSD research increased in the years following World Wars I and II, leading to improved recognition and treatment today.

⌃ Base Hospital 21 staff, ca. 1917
Courtesy of the Becker Medical Library, Washington
University School of Medicine
VC025006

‹ Base Hospital 21 in Rouen, France, ca. 1917
Courtesy of the Becker Medical Library, Washington
University School of Medicine
VC025032

> **Maj. Julia Stimson, ca. 1920**
Library of Congress
LC-DIG-hec-14335

MAJOR JULIA STIMSON, ARMY NURSE CORPS

A St. Louis transplant since age five, Julia Stimson grew interested in medicine during her youth. She went on to receive her nursing degree and became director of the Washington University Training School for Nurses in 1914. Three years later, Stimson joined the Army Nurse Corps and was assigned to Base Hospital 21 as chief nurse. She left the field hospital in April 1918 to take over the Red Cross Nursing Service. Shortly before the end of the war, she became chief nurse of the entire American Expeditionary Force.

After the war, Stimson was the first woman to achieve the rank of major in the US Army. She continued her military service during World War II as part of the Army Nurse Corps.

NURSE MARY STEPHENSON, ARMY NURSE CORPS

Nurse Mary Stephenson was training nurses at Washington University in St. Louis when war broke out. She and 64 other nurses formed the core of Base Hospital 21 from 1917 to 1919. After the war, Nurse Stephenson returned to St. Louis to become supervisor of nurses for the Board of Education. Her wartime service, like that of many nurses overseas, saved thousands of lives.

◀ **Uniform of Nurse Mary Stephenson, ca. 1918**
Missouri Historical Society Collections
1951-043-0001

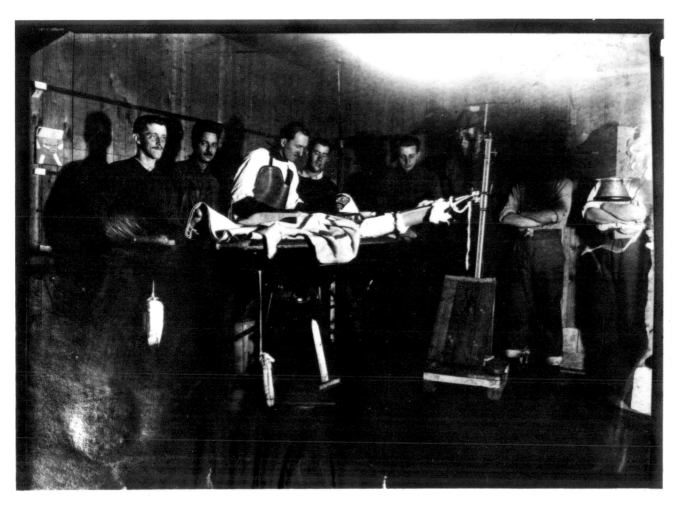

CAPTAIN EDWIN ERNST, BASE HOSPITAL 21

Prior to the war, St. Louis native Dr. Edwin Ernst was director of the radiology department at Washington University in St. Louis. As a doctor at Base Hospital 21, Cpt. Ernst, who was an expert in X-ray technology, built a rudimentary yet effective X-ray machine to examine incoming wounded soldiers. Ernst's machine expedited diagnoses and contributed to the hospital's remarkably low 2 percent death rate.

∧ **Cpt. Edwin Ernst using the X-ray machine he constructed at Base Hospital 21, ca. 1918**
Courtesy of the Saint Louis Science Center
39-09-087.05

> **Glass X-ray slide made by Cpt. Edwin Ernst at Base Hospital 21, ca. 1918**
Courtesy of the Saint Louis Science Center
39-09-087.02

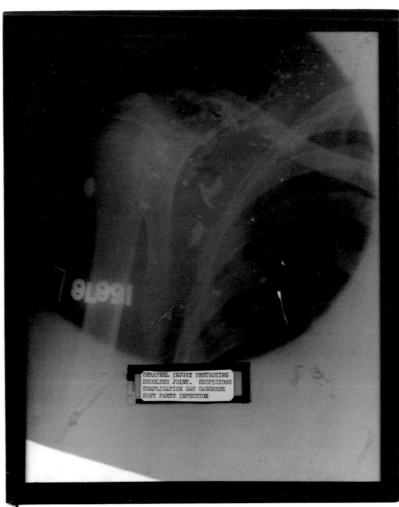

This document is not a passport but is issued with the approval of the Department of State.

UNITED STATES OF AMERICA.

Form No. 633-2—A. G. O.
Ed. Nov. 26-17—3,000.

WAR DEPARTMENT. OF EMBARKATION

CERTIFICATE OF IDENTITY.

Place _HOBOKEN, N. J._

No. _20776_

Date _SEP 3 - 1918_ , 19

I certify that _Esther E. Leonard_ is attached to the sanitary service
(Given name.)   (Surname.)

of the United States Army, is authorized to accompany the _Anaesthetic Unit_
(Designate the organization to which attached.)

_#1_ , in the capacity of _Contract Surgeon_ ,
(Describe function.)

and is entitled to the privileges and immunities provided in Chapter III of the International Red Cross Convention of 1906. A brassard as prescribed in Article 20 thereof, which bears the same number as this certificate, has been issued to the person named. Identification data:

Female   _26_   _Blue_   _Brown_
(Sex.)   (Age.)   (Color of eyes.)   (Color of hair.)

_5' 3"_   _145_   _White_
(Height, approximate.)   (Weight, approximate.)   (Race.)

REMARKS: _None_
(Include here notation of scars, etc., visible when clothed, which will aid in identification.)

C. H. Dayhuff.
(Signature of issuing officer.)

MAJOR, A. G.
Identification Officer
(Rank and title.)

Index finger
right hand.

Tip of finger this end.

Figner print.

Esther E. Leonard.
(Signature of bearer.)

SURGEON ESTHER LEONARD, OPERATING TEAM NO. 158

World War I was a time of many firsts for women, including sending seven women overseas as contract surgeons. One of these women was Dr. Esther Leonard, who had received specialized training in anesthetics at the St. Louis College of Physicians and Surgeons. As part of Operating Team No. 158, Surgeon Leonard helped conduct critical surgeries near the front lines through the end of the war. As evidenced in her poem "Chamber of Horrors," Leonard's experience made a lasting impression on her.

∧ **Surgeon Esther Leonard's military identification papers, ca. 1918**
Missouri Historical Society Collections
A18140-0001

THE CHAMBER OF HORRORS

I went on duty as usual
      At the hour of seven P.M.
To ease the pain and suffering
      Of our gallant wounded men;
They fought thier battles over,
      Mid the dreams of ether's fumes;
Some moan for wife or Mother
      While some of them curse the Huns.

For days they have been in the trenches,
      In dug-outs of mud and mire,
Facing machine guns and cannons,
      Building thier fenches of wire;
O'er No-Mans-Land in the darkness,
      Creeping along kike snails,
Listening to the patter of shrapnel
      Or the machine gun bullet's wail.

Perhaps in the dawn of the morning
      The order will come to advance;
Each man is filled with glory,
      Each man is given his chance
To reckon with any German,
      The Kaiser Crown Prince and all,
He can give him a machine gun bullet,
      Or feed him a rifle ball.

Then when the fighting is over
      And the roll is called again
We know the toll collected,
      From our army of fearless men:
Death is not all the horrors
      To be reckoned with in thei strife,
'Tis those blinded or wounded,
      And left cripples the rest of thier life.

Those that have gone to thier Master,
      Were tenderly laid to rest;
While those that were blinded and mangled
      Were brought to us to be dressed:
Oh! blessed be the word anaesthesia,
      Be it chloroform, ether, cocain,
For in that "Chamber of Horrors"
      It vanishes suffering and pain.   Esther E. Leonard.

                              Written October 18th 1918.
                                 Evac. Hospital #6
                                    Souilly France.

∧ Surgeon Esther Leonard's poem "Chamber of Horrors," ca. 1918
Missouri Historical Society Collections
A1814-00060

CAPTAIN JOHN HARDESTY, SEAFORTH HIGHLANDERS

When Dr. John Hardesty joined the US Medical Corps in June 1917, he likely never imagined his uniform would include a Scottish kilt.

Three years of war had taken a toll on the Allies' medical staff, a crisis that required American doctors to serve in foreign units. Cpt. Hardesty was assigned to the British 51st Division, nicknamed the Seaforth Highlanders. Shortly after he reported for duty, the Germans launched their 1918 spring offensive, and Hardesty was captured near Amiens, France. He spent the remainder of the war in the Rastatt and Villingen prisoner-of-war camps, regularly writing his family in St. Louis and aiding in the successful escape of a fellow prisoner.

◄ Cpt. John Hardesty in his Seaforth Highlanders uniform, ca. 1917
Missouri Historical Society Collections
A2293-00002

⌄ Seaforth Highlanders cap of Cpt. John Hardesty, ca. 1917
Missouri Historical Society Collections
2006-092-0001-003

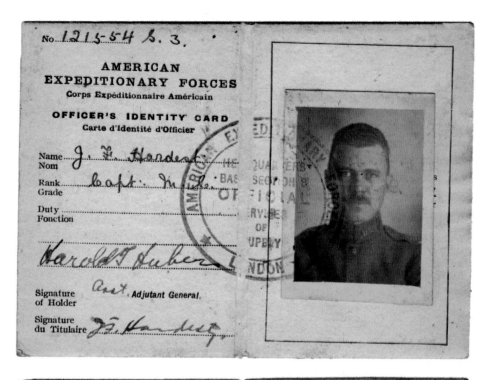

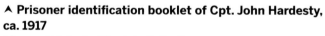

⌃ Prisoner identification booklet of Cpt. John Hardesty, ca. 1917

Missouri Historical Society Collections

A2293-00003

➤ British identification tags of Cpt. John Hardesty, ca. 1917

Missouri Historical Society Collections

2006-092-0024

HELPED COMRADES TO ESCAPE

Dr. Hardesty Aided Fellow Prisoners in German Camp to Liberty.

How Capt. John F. Hardesty, of 3206 California avenue, a medical officer, who returned to St. Louis last February after having been in a German prison camp for nine months, directed a well-formed plan for the escape of American officers from the German prison camp at Villigen, Baden, was related to a Post-Dispatch reporter last week by Lieut. Harold B. Willis, of Boston, member of the Lafayette Escadrille, who lectured at the Principia school. Capt. Hardesty had not told in St. Louis of his part in the escape.

Lieut. Willis who was one of 13 American officers attempted to escape and he and two others were the only ones who succeeded in getting away and reaching the allied lines. The attempt was made Oct. 4, 1918. Since his return to the United States Lieut. Willis has toured the Pacific coast lecturing in support of the Victory Loan and relating the details of his escape.

The success of his effort, he said, was due entirely to the efficient direction of Capt. Hardesty and to the unselfish work of a team of fellow prisoners working under Hardesty. These assistants had no hope of escape, since their part was to give the signals and provide diversions to attract the attention of the guards at the right time. They were risking their lives, Lieut. Willis said, for if their part in the plot had been discovered they probably would have been killed by the Germans.

Lieut. Willis and Lieut. Edouard V. Isaacs, U. S. N., who was captured when a German submarine sank the American transport President Lincoln, May 31, 1918, took the lead in organizing the party of officers who were to make the attempt to escape and Capt. Hardesty undertook to direct the inside work by which the plan was to be put into operation.

The camp was surrounded by two barbed wire fences and a ditch and at night was brilliantly illuminated by powerful electric lamps. These lamps were outside the inclosure and the feed wires, which were bare iron, were far enough from the prison fences that it was thought the prisoners could not interfere with them.

A cordon of guards was maintained around the enclosure day and night, and at night any prisoner seen approaching the wire was likely to be shot. The first concern of the American officers was to devise a means to put out the lights. For this purpose, under Capt. Hardesty's direction, the Americans for two months collected and saved all bits of wire and tin that they could find. Tediously and secretly these were worked into five chains, each about 30 feet long. These chains were to be thrown over the electric light wires to short circuit them and burn out fuses.

Another group of prisoners was organized to throw tin cans and other objects over the fence at certain points in order to divert the attention of the guards from the place where the light wires were to be short circuited.

Lieut. Willis said Capt. Hardesty stationed his men and then gave the signal for the operation to begin by dropping his handkerchief and picking it up three times in succession. This was done under the eyes of German guards, he said.

The metal chains caused all the lights to go out, Lieut. Willis, said, and in the confusion he and his companions undertook the difficult feat of getting through the wire and past the guards. He and the other two who were successful traveled cross country, and reached the Rhine, which they swam, and finally made their way into friendly territory. Lieut. Willis wore a uniform resembling that of the German soldier, which he had made from a Polish uniform.

Lieut. Willis said that as far as he had learned none of the Americans who assisted in the plot was discovered.—Post-Dispatch, Junt 11.

◄ *St. Louis Post-Dispatch* newspaper clipping titled "Helped Comrades to Escape," June 1919
Missouri Historical Society Collections
A2293-00004

SERGEANT MICHAEL ELLIS, COMPANY C, 28TH INFANTRY, 1ST DIVISION

"During the entire day's engagement he operated far in advance of the first wave of his company, voluntarily undertaking most dangerous missions and single-handedly attacking and reducing machine-gun nests . . . at all times showing marked heroism and fearlessness."—Sgt. Michael Ellis, Medal of Honor Citation

Sergeant York of St. Louis. The Lone Wolf. Machine Gun Mike. St. Louis native Michael Ellis earned each of these nicknames in honor of his heroic actions during World War I.

Adopted and raised by a Polish family after his mother died, Ellis quit school at age 12 to work in his father's print shop before enlisting in the Army at age 18. By 1918, Ellis was in France with the rank of sergeant and five years of Army service under his belt.

On October 5 of that year, Sgt. Ellis earned his Lone Wolf moniker by single-handedly capturing dozens of German soldiers and silencing several machine-gun nests. For his extraordinary actions, Ellis was awarded the Medal of Honor.

▲ **Sgt. Michael Ellis, ca. 1918**
St. Louis Post-Dispatch

PART 3
THE HOME FRONT
1917-1919

FOR EVERY ST. LOUISAN ON THE FRONT LINES, THOUSANDS MORE supported the war effort on the home front. Munitions, aircraft, artillery, and war matériel of every kind poured out of St. Louis factories and businesses. New jobs and opportunities brought women and African Americans into the local workforce, along with demands for better working conditions.

Meanwhile, vast propaganda campaigns encouraged sacrifice. Citizens were asked to conserve food for the war effort by canning, gardening, and changing their diets to observe Meatless Mondays and Wheatless Wednesdays. They were also called on to fund the war through the purchase of liberty bonds. St. Louisans responded, and the city regularly exceeded its sales quota.

Wartime propaganda also had a more sinister side, demanding nothing short of absolute loyalty to America and its policies. St. Louis–area Germans were often accused of disloyalty and dissent, tensions that climaxed with the lynching of miner Robert Prager in 1918.

THE ENEMY ON THE HOME FRONT

The war against Germany was fought not only in European trenches but also on American streets. Beginning in 1917, the US government enacted controversial policies that targeted German Americans and political organizations opposed to the war. Among these policies were the Espionage Act, the Sedition Act, and the Trading with the Enemy Act.

St. Louis's large German population came under attack from neighbors as well. Propaganda sowed paranoia throughout the community while rumors of German plots to blow up the Eads Bridge and sabotage riverfront industry spread, prompting armed militias and vigilantes to take matters into their own hands.

CHAPMAN
A. B. FREY
EST C. DONNELL
OTT HANCOCK

50. N. C. COLLIER
51. G. V. R. MECHIN
52. WM. V. O'DONNELL
53. DR. JOS. GRINDON
54. FRANK J. DIRKERS
55. ROB'T. E. BULLOCK
56. L. MC DOUGAN
57. F. E. WILLIAMS
58. ALLEN D. MC KINNEY

59. DR. A. J. MILLER
60. JAS. H. HOSKINS
61. REV. E. J. GALE
62. THOS. L. MAULDIN
63. WM. H. BRONAUGH
64. HENRY H. OBERSCHELP
65. I. LANDAUER
66. A. L. LEVI
67. H N. MORGAN
68. HENRY A. KERSTING
69. HARRY SIMON
70. J. H. GROSSE
71. MYRON R. STURTEVANT
72. ARTHUR P. MEAGHER
73. WM. R. SCHNEIDER
74. JUDGE T. L. ANDERSON
75. SAM'L. A. MITCHELL
76. J. HUGH POWERS
77. OSCAR LEONARD
78. VICTOR LICHTENSTEIN

ernment in informing the
spoken word. on questions
ing enemy propaganda and in
pirational war work of the nation.

OPERATING UNDER AUTHORITY
COMMITTEE
ON PUBLIC INFORMATION

∧ **St. Louis's Four-Minute Men, ca. 1918**
Missouri Historical Society Collections
P0015-00022

Four Minute
Patriotic Addresses
Made in St. Louis Theatres and
Elsewhere on Subjects of
National Importance

Under the

Authority of the Committee
on Public Information
Washington, D.C.

by

G. M. PHILLIPS

Oct. 1917 to June 1918

COMMITTEE ON PUBLIC INFORMATION

"We did not call it propaganda, for that word, in German hands, had come to be associated with deceit and corruption."—George Creel, Head of the Committee on Public Information, 1918

Led by Missouri journalist George Creel, the federal Committee on Public Information was established by executive order in April 1917. Its purpose was to influence public opinion regarding participation in the war. As a result, propaganda permeated every facet of American life. From the theater, to the classroom, to the parlor, Uncle Sam was everywhere. Most visible were the Four-Minute Men, orators who gave four-minute-long presentations on patriotic topics such as food conservation, patriotism, and liberty bonds.

TARGETING GERMANS IN ST. LOUIS

From the first day the country was at war, German Americans received a crystal-clear message: "To Germans Here: Obey the Law and Keep Mouths Shut." Patriotic fervor had gripped the nation, leading to the rise of the civilian-led and government-backed American Protective League, which targeted Germans and any activities deemed unpatriotic.

In St. Louis, German street names were changed. For example, Berlin Ave. became Pershing Ave., and Von Versen Ave. turned into Enright Ave. Germans were also barred from industrial areas of the city to prevent potential sabotage. Meanwhile, the German language was removed from classrooms and censored in newspapers.

‹ Four Minute Patriotic Addresses Made in St. Louis Theatres and Elsewhere on Subjects of National Importance, by G. M. Phillips, ca. 1918
Missouri Historical Society Collections
A1771-00016

› Newspaper clipping showing restricted industrial zones that Germans were not allowed to enter, April 1917
St. Louis Post-Dispatch

ST. LOUIS, SATURDAY EVENING, APRIL 21, 1917—12 PAGES.

St. Louis Districts From Which Enemy Aliens Are Barred

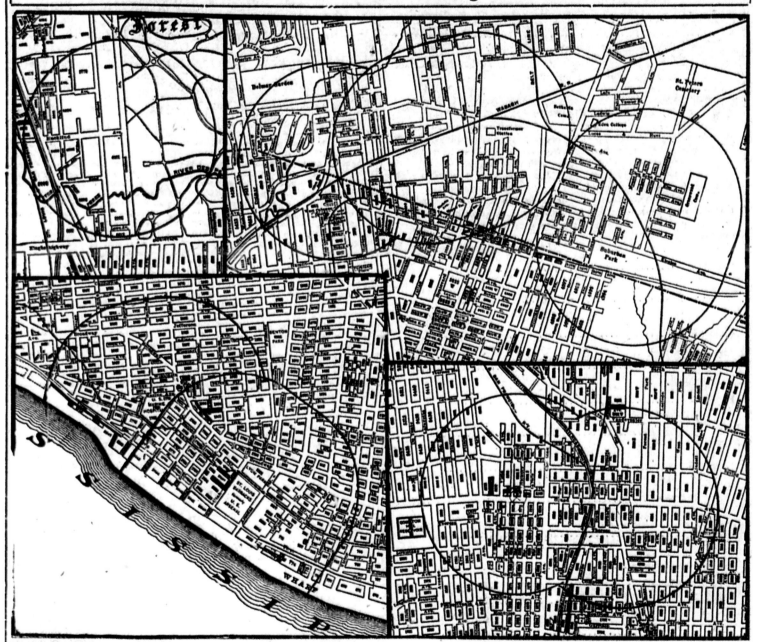

THESE are reproductions from the official government map showing the sections of St. Louis from which all enemy aliens must move. At the upper left hand, the center of the circle is Troop B Armory. At the upper right-hand corner the centers are three large munition factories. At the lower left, the Marine Hospital and the S. Louis Barracks are the centers, and the lower right-hand the armories of Battery A and the First Regiment are the central points.

In April 1918, German immigrant and miner Robert Prager was lynched in Collinsville, Illinois, on false rumors of being a German spy. Eleven men were indicted for his murder, but the jury found them to be innocent. One jury member said of the verdict, "Well, I guess nobody can say we aren't loyal now," reflecting the belief that to be loyal was to be anti-German—even if that meant being complicit in an unjust ruling.

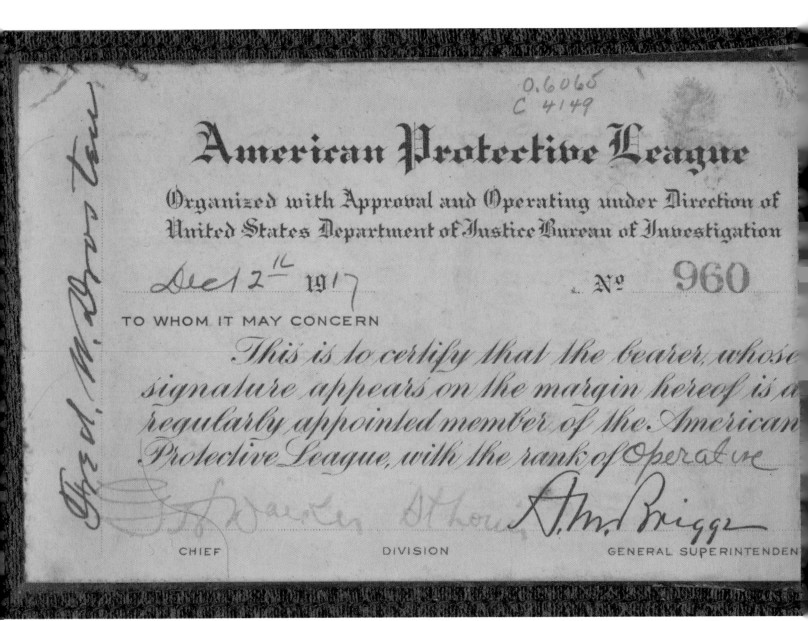

⌃ ⟩ Robert Prager and the men charged with his murder, 1918
St. Louis Post-Dispatch

⟨ American Protective League membership card of Fred Drosten, ca. 1918
Missouri Historical Society Collections
A0410-00002

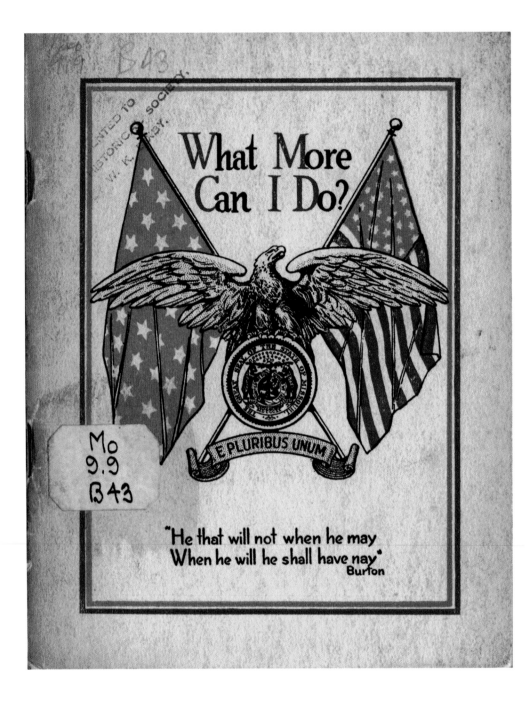

THE MISSOURI HOME GUARD

With the Missouri National Guard deployed, Missouri governor Frederick Gardner allowed for the formation of the Missouri Home Guard to alleviate fears of riots and German saboteurs. Hundreds of businessmen, factory workers, and German Americans seeking to prove their patriotism joined the ranks of the Missouri Home Guard. Armed with decades-old equipment, the group patrolled the streets, paraded, and trained. The men even put on a mock "invasion" of Clayton as part of their exercises.

> **1st Regiment, Missouri Home Guard flag and detail of center, ca. 1918**
Missouri Historical Society Collections
X11047

◂ ⌄ Missouri Home Guard recruiting pamphlet, ca. 1918
Missouri Historical Society Collections
GRA00239, GRA00240, GRA0041

44   WHAT MORE CAN I DO?

is but natural, and this loyalty soon extends to loyalty in general.

When you say a man is loyal, the world considers that you have paid him a high tribute.

In the military service order and system are watchwords. The smooth running of the military machine depends on them.

The care and attention that the soldier is required to give at all times to his clothes, accouterments, equipment and other belongings, instill in him habits of orderliness.

Orderliness increases the value of a man.

Self-confidence is founded on one's ability to do things. The soldier is taught to defend himself with his rifle, and to take care of himself and to do things in almost any sort of a situation, all of which gives him confidence in himself — SELF-CONFIDENCE.

Respect for constituted authority, which is a part of the soldier's creed, teaches him respect for himself — SELF-RESPECT.

Self-confidence and self-respect are a credit to any man.

Guard duty, outpost duty, patrolling, scouting and target practice, train both the eye and the mind to observe.

Power of observation is a valuable faculty for a man to possess.

In drilling, patrolling, marching, maneuvers and in other phases of his training and instruction, the soldier is taught the principles of team-work — co-operation — whose soul is LOYALTY, a trait of every good soldier.

Team-work — co-operation — leads to success in life.

The cardinal habit of the soldier is obedience. To obey orders and regulations is a habit with the soldier. And this habit of obeying orders and regulations teaches him to heed law and order.

WHAT MORE CAN I DO?   45

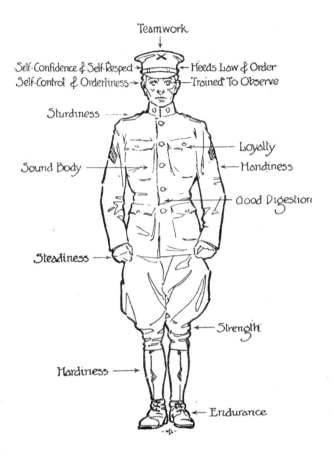

DO YOU MEASURE UP TO HIM?

St. Louis, Mo. April 15, 1918.

TO ALL MEMBERS OF FIRST REGIMENT, MISSOURI HOME GUARD:

The Liberty Loan Organization have provided sales committees to solicit the large industries and corporations and their officers and employes, in the City. Even though orders have been issued to the contrary, there has been confusion caused by members of the Regiment competing with the sales committees referred to.

In this connection, your attention is called to the following letter, which you will please observe in your solicitation for subscriptions -- a list of the exempted businesses and industries is now on file at your Company headquarters:

"Col. McBride:-

Following the conversation which we had with you, and the lists of certain industries and businesses which were handed you this morning - which for want of a better name we will refer to as 'exempted businesses and industries' - we would request that for the present the Home Guard of St. Louis make no solicitation for the sale of Liberty Loan Bonds of any of the firms or industries on this so-called exempted list, either of the firms themselves, the officers or others in control of these firms, or the employees of these firms.

Except for the industries so listed, we hope that the Home Guard will continue the splendid work they have started and which they are so capable of doing.

We would, however, very much appreciate it if, during the last ten days of the campaign, the Home Guard would extend their work of solicitation for the sale of the bonds to these exempted firms and their officers and employees.

Very truly yours,
(Signed) W.D.Dean, Jr.
GENERAL SALES MANAGER, METROPOLITAN DISTRICT
LIBERTY LOAN COMMITTEE."

You will note the words of appreciation Mr. Dean has said of our work. In the first eight days of the campaign this Regiment had received 2,243 subscriptions amounting to $508,600. Can we not do this each of the three remaining weeks of the campaign and reach the remarkable total of $2,000,000? You individually can answer this.

In any event, the Government, the Liberty Loan Committee, and your officers are proud and happy of the remarkable showing you make and that we know you are going to make. Company E and Company B have reached Berlin. Company F has landed in France.

1st Regiment MISSOURI HOME GUARDS
LIBERTY LOAN COMMITTEE.

MISSOURI HOME GUARD
1st REGIMENT

ST. LOUIS

Sep. 13, 1917.

FROM   HEADQUARTERS CO. "H".

TO

SUBJECT   The following Regulations will be strictly enforced.

1. All privates and non-commissioned officers will wear only the standard canvas leggings. No other will be permitted.

2. No neck-ties can be worn with uniform at drill or when on duty.

3. The sleeves of shirts must never be rolled up nor cuffs turned back. It is permissable to unbutton the top button of the shirt if desired.

4. These regulations are prescribed for the entire regiment and will be strictly enforced in this company.

By order of

Captain Robert H. Gross,
Commanding.

◀ **Circular about solicitation of liberty bonds, April 1918**
Missouri Historical Society Collections
A0258-00005

⌃ **Regulations for Company H, 1st Regiment, Missouri Home Guard, 1917**
Missouri Historical Society Collections
A0258-00004

Company 'H'

They may say what they please
They may shivver and freeze
But in any good drill
Company 'H' heads the bill

In shooting we're best
With marksmen we're blest
You may make a safe bet
We will go fifty yet

The kaiser may use ~~any~~
Anymmeans he may choose
But if he comes here
We will chase him a year

When trouble does burst
To stop it we're first
When bullets do whiz
We show them the biz.

I

Hoorah for H. Company, fellows,
    For the officers and its men too;
Let's get out and work like the devil,
    And learn every maneuver that's new.

II

At roll call let every man answer,
    With a good ringing, echoing, here.
So if in the future we're needed,
    Our Captain will have nothing to fear.

III

If they'd send us to France with the Sammies,
    We'd show them how H. Company fight;
We'd hold our line with the best ones,
    And go after our enemies right.

IV

We would knock the I out of Kaiser,
    We would capture the Crown Prince so fine;
With our officers brave and so handsome,
    We would smash old Hindenburg's line.

V

So let every fellow get busy,
    And keep his mind on the race,
So when the order is left oblique,
    We won't make it squads right face.

(Tune Tipperary)

THE HOME GUARDS.
(CHORUS)

If there's trouble, you've got the Home Guards

We can take care of you

If the Kaiser, should take a notion

To cause trouble over here

He'll find—he's mistaken

Cause we are prepared

We will give our lives, if they are needed

For the U.S.A.

"While we are Canning the Kaiser"

1.

Bring the good old bugle boys, we'll sing another song,
    Sing it with a spirit that will move the world
        along,
Sing it as we need to sing it, half a million strong,
    While we are canning the Kaiser.

Chorus:

Oh Bill! Oh Bill! We're on the job today,
    Oh Bill! Oh Bill! We'll seal you so you'll stay
We'll put you up with ginger in the good old Yankee way,
    While we are canning the Kaiser.

11.

Hear the song we're singing on the shining road to France
    Hear the Tommies and see the Poilus prance,
Africanders and Konucks, and Scots with shining lance,
    While we are canning the Kaiser.

111.

Bring the guns from Bethlehem by way of old New York,
    Bring the beans from Boston and don't leave out the
        pork,
Bring a load of soda pop and pull the grape juice cork
    While we are canning the Kaiser.

1V.

Come you men from Dixie land, you lumber jacks from Maine,
    Come you Texas cowboys, and you farmers of the plaine
        From Florida and Oregon, we boast the Yankee strain,
    While we are canning the Kaiser.

V.

Now we're started on the job, we mean to put it thru-
    Ship the kings and Kaisers all, and make the world anew,
Clear the way for common folk, for men like me and you,
    While we are canning the Kaiser-

M. J. Grossman
Co. H.

∧ ➤ **Songs of Company H, 1st Regiment, Missouri Home Guard, ca. 1917**
Missouri Historical Society Collections
A0258-00003

Home Guard Company Will Be on Duty at Armory During Strike

Units to Take Turns on Guard Ready, if Required, to Quell Riot.

One company of the First Regiment, Home Guards, is on duty at the Armory on Grand avenue all day and night to render service in the event Gov. Gardner calls upon them for aid in the street car strike.

The plan for mobilizing one company of the Home Guards is the idea of Col. Philip B. Fouke, who said the drill would be of great benefit to the members of each company. Since the plan was put into effect at noon Sunday two companies have been on duty. A different company will remain on guard at the Armory for twenty-four hours at a time, when it will be relieved by another company.

Men Are Given Sweaters.

Company I, Capt. N. K. Givens, commanding, was the first one called out. The men responded, and before they had been on duty for an hour Mrs. Frank V. Hammar, chairman of the St. Louis branch of the Red Cross, had provided sweaters, helmets, blankets, socks and other warm clothing for the men, as well as cots. All of the members of the two companies who have been called out praise the Red Cross.

The duty of the men is to guard the Armory property and to take advantage of their assemblage to drill. None of the men leave the Armory while on guard duty. None of the men will be permitted to do anything but guard duty except upon the direction of the governor, said Lieut. Selden P. Spencer, battalion adjutant.

Only One Fails to Respond.

When Company H, Capt. Robert H. Gross, commanding, was called on duty at 12 o'clock yesterday for a twenty-four hour watch 113 of the 114 members of the company responded.

Another company, probably Company L, will go on duty at noon today. Col. Fouke has set no time within which this guard duty and drill will end, but it is probable it will be continued indefinitely.

Since the first orders were issued a rivalry has started among the companies as to which will furnish the largest number of men. The fact that only one man failed to respond to the summons for Company H is considered remarkable.

◄ *St. Louis Globe-Democrat* newspaper clipping titled "Home Guard Company Will Be on Duty at Armory During Strike," ca. 1918
Missouri Historical Society Collections
A0258-00002

ST. LOUIS INDUSTRY AND LABOR

The war created an industrial boom in St. Louis and the nation. Companies across the city, including Wagner Electric and Scullin Steel, produced war matériel. Across the river in East St. Louis, Illinois, stockyards bustled with activity as mules, horses, and other Missouri livestock were prepared to be sent overseas, where they would pull wagons, artillery, and ambulances.

▲ **Wagner Electric strike, May 1918**
Missouri Historical Society Collections
N39388

WAGNER ELECTRIC MANUFACTURING COMPANY

Wagner Electric, located in Wellston, Missouri, produced munitions for Great Britain and Russia prior to American entry into the war. With its machinery already geared toward producing munitions, Wagner Electric was among the first companies in the country to be issued a government contract. It produced depth charges, artillery shells, naval guns, and other artillery parts until the war's end.

By 1918, 25 percent of Wagner Electric's workforce was composed of women. That same year, Wagner's female employees led a successful strike against the company for shorter workdays and better wages.

⌃ **Women inspecting fuse bodies at Wagner Electric,
ca. 1917**
Missouri Historical Society Collections
P0244-K0627-8g

"A most magnificent creature," replied a British Brigadier when asked for an opinion of the lowly American mule. "And he has a much better character than generally is given to him. He is something like a camel in that respect. Most people cry down and berate the poor old camel, but once you get to know him he is much to be admired. It is just the same with the mule."—Cornell Daily Sun, February 16, 1917

MISSOURI MULES AND HORSES

Though technological innovations dominated World War I, the unreliability of trucks and automobiles in battlefield conditions caused armies to rely on mules and horses to move equipment. The Missouri mule gained international renown for its wartime contributions. Livestock companies across the state supplied mules to the French and British armies early in the war, and they later did the same for the US Army. The Missouri mule was named the official state animal in 1995.

⌃ Members of the 137th Ambulance Company putting a gas mask on a mule, 1918
Courtesy of the National World War I Museum and Memorial, Kansas City, Missouri, U.S.A.
1981.16.65

⌄ Four-mule escort wagon of the type produced by the American Car and Foundry Co. St. Charles plant, ca. 1918
Missouri Historical Society Collections
P0229-01118

⌄ Artillery caisson of the type produced by the American Car and Foundry Co. St. Charles plant, ca. 1918
Missouri Historical Society Collections
P0229-01095

AMERICAN CAR AND FOUNDRY COMPANY

Before World War I, the American Car and Foundry Company's plant in St. Charles, Missouri, produced wooden passenger railcars and streetcars. Because it was equipped for substantial woodworking, the St. Charles plant was tasked with building 50,000 Army escort wagons, crates for artillery implements, and caissons.

SCULLIN STEEL

One of the largest steel companies in the world during World War I was St. Louis's Scullin Steel. Located at 6700 Manchester Rd., Scullin Steel operated 11 open-hearth furnaces. It produced cast-steel slugs as well as cast-steel ingots for 2.5-, 8-, and 9.5-inch artillery shells. The company also housed a US Army Ordnance Department warehouse on nearby Ecoff Ave. for storing artillery-shell components.

⋀ **Pouring artillery-shell ingots at Scullin Steel, ca. 1918**
Missouri Historical Society Collections
N22374

> **View of Ecoff Ave. with sign for US Army Ordnance Department warehouse visible, July 1919**
Missouri Historical Society Collections
N08322

▾ **Foundry Plant #1 at Scullin Steel, ca. 1918**
Missouri Historical Society Collections
N28216

ANHEUSER-BUSCH

When the United States joined the war in 1917, Anheuser-Busch found itself in a difficult situation. German ties had prompted the company to invest in German war bonds while America had remained diplomatically neutral. To combat charges of disloyalty after the United States declared war on Germany, business owner August Busch immediately canceled all outstanding contracts for his Busch-Sulzer Brothers Diesel Engine Company and began producing submarine engines for the US Navy. On the brewing side of things, Anheuser-Busch converted its labels from German to English.

Through 1918, Anheuser-Busch contributed millions of dollars to the war effort through liberty bonds and donations to war work. The company loaned its Bevo Boat for military recruitment drives and leased floor space in the Bevo Building for munitions storage. August Busch even went so far as to begin converting Anheuser-Busch to a munitions factory, but the war ended before the conversion could be completed.

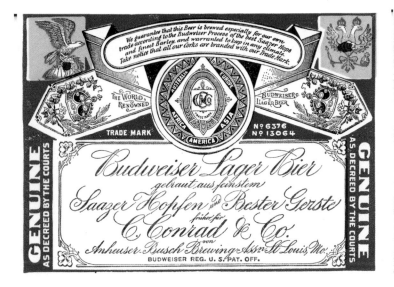

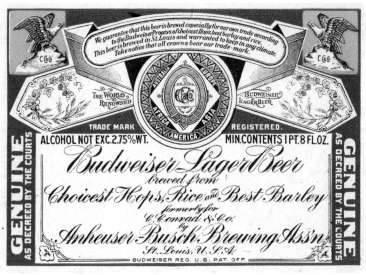

◄ **Postcard showing Bevo Boat with soldiers, 1918**
Anheuser-Busch

▼ **St. Louis Aircraft Corporation factory with JN-4D "Jenny" planes outside, ca. 1918**
Greater St. Louis Air and Space Museum
GSTLASM.0001

ST. LOUIS AIRCRAFT CORPORATION

The St. Louis Aircraft Corporation was established in 1917 as a collaborative effort between the St. Louis Car Company and the Huttig Sash and Door Company. It became one of six contractors to produce the Curtiss JN-4D "Jenny" aircraft, which was used to train pilots across the country.

◄ **Budweiser beer label in German, 1886–1908**
Anheuser-Busch

◄ **Budweiser beer label in English, 1918–1920**
Anheuser-Busch

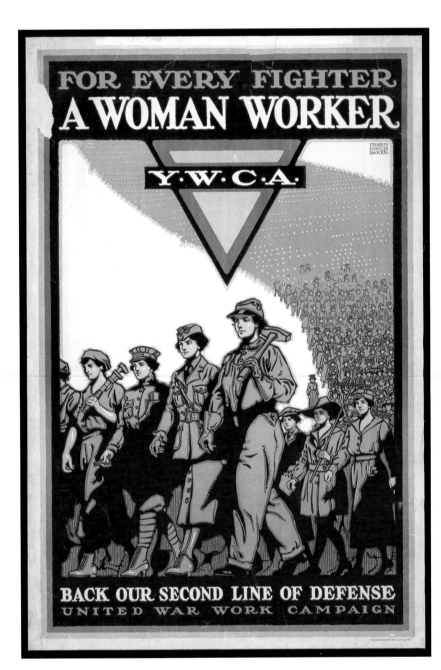

∧ Poster promoting women's war work, ca. 1918
Library of Congress
LC-DIG-ppmsca-40823

CHANGING WORKFORCE

World War I was a time of great change in America's workforce. To fulfill wartime contracts and offset the loss of millions of men recruited into the military, businesses turned to women and African Americans. New workers meant new demands, which led to labor strikes for better working conditions, including the 1918 strike at
St. Louis–based Wagner Electric.

Many of these new workers would lose their jobs in the years following the war, as millions of servicemen returned to the workforce. However, the wartime gains made by female workers in particular persisted and created new opportunities in the postwar years.

WOMEN WORK THEIR WAY UP

The war afforded new opportunities to St. Louis's women and contributed to the already growing suffrage movement. As men enlisted in the military, women were recruited to fill the jobs they left behind. These higher-paying positions led to the emergence of a new class of largely white, single, and independent women.

African Americans and immigrants filled the jobs these women left behind, working as domestic helpers, laundresses, and seamstresses. Their wages also increased.

∨ Women working on detonator sockets at Wagner Electric, ca. 1917
Missouri Historical Society Collections
N23907

AFRICAN AMERICANS IN INDUSTRY AND THE 1917 EAST ST. LOUIS RACE RIOT

The war created many job opportunities in St. Louis and East St. Louis, which attracted African American workers to the region. Business owners could get away with paying these new arrivals lower wages than their white counterparts, so they used them as replacement workers in the steel, railroad, and manufacturing industries.

In East St. Louis, white concerns over jobs and heightened racial tensions boiled over into a full-fledged race riot on July 2, 1917. White rioters burned more than 200 African American homes and left more than 600 black people homeless. Another 40 to 200 black people were killed in the riot, and even more fled across the Mississippi River to St. Louis in search of safety. The incident gained nationwide attention and prompted marches across the country.

∧ **African American workers moving a crucible of molten metal at Scullin Steel, ca. 1917**
Missouri Historical Society Collections
N22392

∧ **Fire near the East St. Louis Public Library at 8th and Broadway during the race riot, July 1917**
Missouri Historical Society Collections
N26005

Official Organ of the Supreme Lodge Committee Knights of Pythias N. A., S. A., E., A., A. & A.

The St. Louis Argus

VOL. VI. NO. 12   ST. LOUIS, MO., FRIDAY, JULY 6, 1917.   PRICE 5 CENTS

RIOT A NATIONAL DISGRACE

✦✦✦✦✦✦   ✦✦✦✦✦✦   ✦✦✦✦✦✦   ✦✦✦✦✦✦

East St. Louis Shrouds Country In Shame. Mob Commits Most Atrocious Crimes On Innocent Negroes While Police and Militiamen Look On With Apathy. President Called On To Stop Mob Violence. War Department Asked To Take Hand In Investigation.

NEGROES DID NOT START TROUBLE

Outbreak Caused By White Men In Automobile Shooting Into Negro Homes Sunday Night. Policemen Mistaken For Rioters Are Slain.

Friday morning July 6, the East St. Louis situation, so far as the riot is concerned, seems to be quiet. No further racial trouble is expected. Lawyer N. W. Parden and city detective James Hardiman. Negroes are under arrest charged with neglect of duty. No other state, or city officials have been arrested. A guardsman killed a white man last night, who failed to halt when commanded to do so.

The entire country has been aroused to a sense of shame and pity by the magnitude of the national disgrace enacted by the blood-thirsty rioters in East St. Louis Monday, July 2.

So much has been said in the daily press about the affair, that it would be a waste of time to review the facts in to such depths of savagery and committed such atrocious crimes.

The statements of the daily press about the cruelty to the Negroes administered by the blood-thirsty mob and the laxity of the police and militia were not exaggerated. While our reporter states that there were no less than one hundred Negro men, women and children shot, tortured and burned to death, he believes there were more. How many, no one may ever know. More than two hundred homes were destroyed, with all their contents. The scene of the destruction of life and property was not in the thickly populated district. The mob was too cowardly to invade it, but vented its fury on isolated spots and helpless victims. It had no choice. It was as a sporting

THOUSANDS LEAVE EAST ST. LOUIS CARED FOR HERE

NATIONAL ASSOCIATION FOR ADVANCEMENT OF COLORED PEOPLE, LEADS IN GIVING RELIEF TO THE SUFFERERS.

Red Cross, City Officials, Y. W. C. A., Y. M. C. A. and Hundreds of Noble Citizens of St. Louis Lend Aid, Food, Clothing and Lodging being Provided.

Negroes Begged to Return. Plants Must Close if They Cannot Get Colored Help. Very Few Are Going South.

Thousands of refugees have been fleeing from East St. Louis since Sunday night. The majority have crossed the river into St. Louis and hundreds went immediately to Union Station where they took trains to other cities, in most instances turning a deaf ear to the call from the south. The Big Four Railroad is taking many east to work on the company lines and several large establishments in St. Louis are offering employment.

Agents of the freight houses on the East Side came over Thursday and begged the men to return, guaranteeing protection, but there was no inclination on the part of the men to . . .

a large number of citizens furnished their automobiles to bring the refugees from the bridges. Some few started in to charge the unfortunates but these were . . . disposed of. Among those who . . . tendered their machines are: Chas. . . . Tom Turpin, Richard Kent, Geo. Scott, Jake McAfee, Langston Harrison, Bismark Lavin, Chas. McDonald, Ernest A. Harris, J. H. Harris, Prof. and Mrs. Malone, Chas. McDonald, Miss Emma Nash, and others whose names were not obtained.

George Wright also has rendered valuable assistance with his auto-bus.

The ministers opened all the churches for an overflow from the lodging house, but as many of the citizens have kindly taken hundreds to their homes, the churches have not been needed.

The Young Women's Christian Association, under Miss Belcher, and the Y. M. C. A., led by Mr. Jones, have done noble work.

Mrs. Malone and a corps of workers have been on duty at the Union Station. The Booker Washington Theater has been held in readiness to accommodate all who needed sleeping quarters and through the kindness of Jerry Renfro, and the assistance of Chief Young and Mr. Schmoll, a rest room for men has been opened at 2218 Market St., with benches from the park department.

RELIEF FUNDS PAYABLE TO N.A.A.C.P.

Dyer To Demand An Inquiry Into East Side Riot

Washington, D. C., July 4.—Representative L. C. Dyer, of St. Louis, announced tonight that he would introduce in the House a resolution calling upon the President to direct the Secretary of War to send an army officer to East St. Louis to investigate conditions there and report whether the Illinois authorities were capable of protecting life and property in the event of a continuance of a recurrence of the race riots.

Mr. Dyer expressed the opinion that the President has the power in time of war to use the armed forces of the Federal Government to put down riots whenever the state authorities show their inability to cope with the situation. He charged that Illinois had demonstrated it could not protect either life or property in East St. Louis, and contended the President should take control.

The St. Louis Congressman said it was a disgrace that a great state like Illinois should have permitted the outrages of the last few days in East St. Louis, and asserted it was subject to the condemnation that had been heaped upon Southern states which had failed to stop lynchings.

"I understand," said Mr. Dyer, "that Gen. Barry, commander of the Central Department of the Army, asked . . .

LAWYER WARNS CHICAGO NEGROES TO ARM SELVES

FORMER PROSECUTOR FERDINAND L. BARNETT, SEES DANGER OF RIOTS IN WINDY CITY. CONDEMNS GOV. LOWDEN AND OTHER PUBLIC OFFICIALS FOR RIOTS DUE TO "LAXNESS OF DUTY."

Special to the Argus:—

Chicago, Ill., July 5. The following is an extract of an article which appeared in the Chicago Daily Tribune, issue July 4.

"Arm yourselves now with guns and pistols," said Ferdinand L. Barnett, a former assistant state's attorney, in speaking to 100 Negro men at a mass meeting held last night to protest against the riots and bloodshed in East St. Louis. The meeting took place at 3005 South State Street.

"Don't buy an arsenal," continued Barnett, "but get enough guns to protect yourselves. You may be victims of murders and outrages as have taken place in East St. Louis. And when trouble starts let us not hesitate to call upon our Negro militiamen to defend us."

Condemn State Officials

Barnett and A. H. Roberts, another

▲ St. Louis Argus newspaper clipping titled "Riot a National Disgrace," July 1917
Missouri Historical Society Collections
N27305

ORGANIZING THE HOME FRONT

As soldiers trained and shipped out overseas, organizations throughout the United States launched initiatives to support the war on the home front. The Missouri Council of Defense was established to organize war work in the state, directing efforts to conserve food; sell liberty bonds; and coordinate the contributions of the YMCA, Salvation Army, and American Red Cross at the state level. The city directly supported St. Louisans overseas by sending care packages, knitting, making bandages, and raising funds.

⌃ *Mother Goose in War Time* cover, ca. 1918
Missouri Historical Society Collections
GRA00182

➤ "Rub-a-Dub-Dub" nursery rhyme revised to denounce draft dodgers, German sympathizers, and food wasters, ca. 1918
Missouri Historical Society Collections
GRA00181

⌃ "Little Miss Muffet" nursery rhyme revised to encourage children to buy war-savings thrift stamps, ca. 1918
Missouri Historical Society Collections
GRA00183

MISSOURI COUNCIL OF DEFENSE

In April 1917, Governor Gardner called for the formation of the Missouri Council of Defense, which became the coordinating body between the federal government and Missouri citizens during the war. The council had more than 11,000 members from the state level all the way down to the township level.

The Women's Committee of the Missouri Council of Defense was the state's chief organizing body operating at the state, county, and city levels. It oversaw the distribution of information and publications about food conservation, fundraising, employment, and propaganda through its "patriotic education" division. One such publication was *Mother Goose in War Time,* a collection of traditional nursery rhymes with wartime messages.

Rub-a-dub dub,
Three men in a tub
And who do you think they be?
The slacker, the traitor
The wilful food waster,
—Send them to Germany!

AMERICAN RED CROSS, ST. LOUIS CHAPTER

The American Red Cross was perhaps the most vital war work organization during World War I, providing supplies and medical relief both overseas and at home. Members of the St. Louis chapter, which was founded in 1917, knit socks, mittens, and scarves for troops overseas. They also sent "ditty bags" containing notes of encouragement, candy, and cigarettes to soldiers, including Pvt. Edwin Oberg, a St. Louisan in the 89th Infantry Division.

⌃ **American Red Cross canteen in St. Louis, ca. 1918**
Soldiers Memorial Military Museum Collections
SMX02620-050

➢ **Red Cross ditty bag of Pvt. Edwin Oberg, ca. 1918**
Missouri Historical Society Collections
1982-083-0005

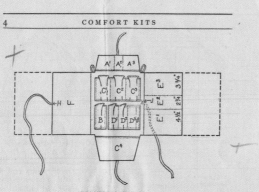

COMFORT KIT No. 2
Fig. 2. Arrangement of articles in Comfort Kit No. 2

A-1 and A-3. Thread, heavy white, and waxed, khaki-color, sometimes called carpet or button thread (wound on cards). On the outside of these pockets attach six khaki-color buttons, size for uniforms, six khaki-color buttons, shirt size, and six white buttons for underwear. Kits intended for the navy should have black thread and buttons instead of the khaki-colored.

A-2. Needles, assorted, large sizes, in case; thimble, large size, celluloid; a piece of sewing wax.

B. Tobacco pouch and tobacco.

C-1. Tooth-powder in tin container, toothbrush.

C-2. Folding-knife and spoon.

C-3. Soap in metal or celluloid box.

C-4. Wash-cloth.

On the outside of this pocket pin 12 No. 3 black safety pins and 6 khaki-color patent trouser-buttons.

D-1. Shaving-brush.

D-2. Shaving-soap.

D-3. Comb, metal, in case.

D-4. Pipe.

E-1. Playing cards or game; cigarette papers.

E-2. Mouth-organ.

E-3. Safety razor and blades.

F. Writing materials, pencil, name and address of donor, handkerchiefs, two or three (khaki-color), and pair of heavy socks, either hand or machine knitted.

Fig. 2a. Showing dimensions for cutting

COMFORT KIT No. 2. *Directions for Making*

Material: One-half yard of goods 36 inches wide; four yards of tape for binding; one small American flag to be sewed on the outside of kit. These flags can be purchased cheaply in the form of ribbon, about twenty-four flags to the yard.

If the material measures only 33 inches, it need not alter the dimensions of the kit except by making the pockets E1–E3, and F proportionately smaller.

Cut out sections A, B, C, and D as indicated on Figure No. 2a. From these pieces make the applied pockets of the case, some flat, others slightly full, as shown on Figure 2.

    Section A: use for pockets marked A1–A3 laid on Flap No. 1
    Section B: use for pocket marked B
    Section C: use for the series of 3 pockets marked C1–C3
    Section D: use, in part, for pocket marked C-4 on Flap No. 2,
    the balance, for pockets marked D1–D4

Fold in selvage ends of goods to form series of pockets marked E1–E3 and large pocket marked F. Bind all edges neatly with stout tape. Attach ties of tape to Flaps 1 and 2 so they can be brought together and tied over the pockets. Attach ties of tape to outside of case at H and J. These ties should be long enough to go twice around kit and keep all secure; two loops of tape should be added as shown in Figure No. 2, that the whole kit may be hung up evenly balanced.

It is important that the openings of the pocket B, and of the C and D series face the loops, so that small articles will not fall out when the case is hung. Snappers sewn at the edge of the pockets E1–E3 and F will help to make their contents more secure.

In general the proportions of the pockets are suggested in the diagrams but no special measurements can be given for them as the size of articles will vary somewhat in different localities and judgment must be ⸻ make the compartments fit the things they are intended to conta⸻

COMFORT KIT No. 3
(For hospital use)

CONTENTS

A.   Writing materials

B-1. Pencil

B-2. Puzzles

B-3. Cigarette paper

B-4. Pipe

B-5. Tobacco and pouch

C-1. Mirror, metal

C-2. Handkerchiefs

C-3. Playing-cards and game

D-1. Comb

D-2. Tooth-paste

D-3. Tooth-brush

D-4. Soap

D-5. Wash-cloth

Safety pins may be attached to the outside of any of these pockets, or on the flap at the back, but sewing materials will probably not be needed much in a hospital.

Frederick Palmer says in *Collier's:* "The men who are fighting for you at the front live from mail to mail." The wounded man especially needs the cheer of a sensible, kindly letter. Put one into your hospital kit. Make it short, make it cheerful, above all make it bespeak your patriotism and appeal to his.

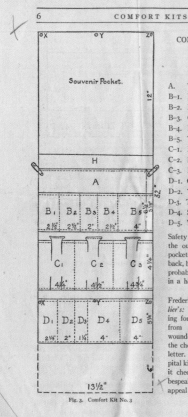

Fig. 3. Comfort Kit No. 3

DIRECTIONS FOR MAKING

This kit is especially designed to be pinned to the side of a bed and to contain the small things which a wounded man will want to keep near him.

Material: Two yards of 33 to 36-inch goods will make three kits 11 to 12 inches wide, or two yards of 27-inch goods will make two kits 13½ inches wide. The latter is probably the better width but the others will be acceptable; two and one-half yards of tape are needed for binding and tie-ends. A piece of stork-sheeting 9 × 13½ inches is required to line the lowest pockets which are for toilet articles which may be damp.

To make the kit, measure and tear the entire strip of goods lengthwise to the width desired. Then tear sidewise from the strip the following pieces for the pockets, as shown in Figure 3:

1. *Pocket A:* 7¼ inches torn will be 6½ inches finished. Three-fourths of an inch has been allowed for turning in at the bottom of the pockets and a narrow hem at the top.

2. *Pockets B1–B5:* 4 inches torn will be 3¼ inches finished.

3. *Full pockets C1–C3:* Two strips 5 inches torn, 4¼ inches finished, the extra fullness is needed to make the pleats. If preferred, piecing the goods for this series of pockets may be avoided by tearing two 5-inch strips off the full width of the material before dividing it lengthwise for the rest of the kits.

To make the pockets marked D1–D5, face the lower end of the long strip of goods with the 9-inch piece of stork-sheeting, sewing both sides of the sheeting firmly to the kit before hemming and turning up the flap which can then be divided into the pockets as indicated in Figure 3.

Hem the upper end of the strips for C1–C3, pleat them and attach to kit case one inch above pockets D1–D5. Hem the strips intended for pockets A and B and apply B to A, sewing the partition seams in B before attaching both pockets at once to kit case, one inch above pockets marked C.

Souvenir pocket: Almost every soldier has a little collection of souvenirs, often including the bullet or piece of shell which has brought him to the hospital. The big pocket of this kit marked "Souvenir Pocket" is intended to hold these and other personal effects. To make this pocket, hem the upper end of the strip of which the kit is made, and fold over a flap 12 inches when finished. While in use this large flap-pocket is turned back and hangs behind the bag, but if the soldier wishes to take his kit with him on leaving the hospital, its contents can be made secure by bringing the flap forward over the small pockets and fastening it down by clips sewed to x, y, and z. The whole kit can then be rolled up and tied as the contents permit. Bind the side edges of the kit securely with the tape and attach

◄ **Instructions on how to make "comfort kits" and knit socks, ca. 1917**
Missouri Historical Society Collections
A1248-00004, A1248-00003

➤ ***Rhymes of a Red Cross Man***, 1916
Missouri Historical Society Collections
A0129-00048

Red Cross
BY N. WALTER MACINTYRE

• • • •

Red Cross, Red Cross
Everyone should come across

• • • •

That may seem like slang to you,
But if so, 'tis nothing new;
Everyone his best must do,
    Red Cross—Red Cross.

War is here, and war is there;
Darkness deep where all was fair;
Death on land, and sea, and air;
    Red Cross—Red Cross.

What a fearful, dreadful loss;
If the Germans get across;
Fate is now at pitch and toss;
    Red Cross—Red Cross.

See, in frenzied battle line,
Son of yours, and son of mine;
See behind, the aid divine,
    Red Cross—Red Cross.

Give, oh give, for mercy's sake;
Give, the German curse to break;
Give, the sufferer's thirst to slake;
    Red Cross—Red Cross.

Some must go, and some must stay;
Some must suffer, some must pay;
Do your duty—now—today!
    Red Cross—Red Cross.

1917
December 17

Louis Globe-Democrat.

8000 Pack Coliseum in Drive to Get 10,000,000 New Red Cross Members

Military Bands Play Patriotic Airs and Prominent Citizens Explain Great Good Organization Is Doing for Country.

The enlistment in St. Louis before Christmas of 500,000 soldiers of mercy—members of the American Red Cross—began last night at a mass meeting of the combined churches of the city at the Coliseum. Several thousand memberships were obtained.

No demonstration in St. Louis since America entered the war has had a deeper tinge of patriotism than last night's Red Cross meeting. In fact, nothing but patriotism could have kept nearly 8000 persons for three hours on a winter night in an auditorium heated only by the fires of loyalty. The "fireman" was W. E. Bilheimer and the fuel was patriotic and appealing speeches, songs and music.

The crowd began to assemble at 6:30 p. m. and at 7 o'clock the Jefferson Barracks Band gave a concert. An hour later the Home Guards marched in to martial strains of music by their band.

The Pageant Choral Society, directed by Frederick Fischer, opened the meeting with a sacred selection, after which Harry F. Knight, director of the St. Louis campaign, introduced George W. Simmons, manager of the Southwestern Division of the American Red Cross.

Tells of Work in France.

Simmons described the work the Red Cross was doing in France. He said that the work the American Red Cross has done there has meant more to that nation than an army of 500,000 soldiers. Of Germany, he said we have all come to understand German philosophy, and declared that through her broken treaties, Germany had evoked the distrust of the world.

"And," he said, "when the treaty of peace is finally signed, it will not bear the signature of William of Hohenzollern."

Simmons said that many believed that because St. Louis has a large so-called German-American population, there was doubt that the Red Cross membership campaign would be backward, "but," he said, "I don't believe it. Our people here in St. Louis are first of all Americans, and if there are any who are not, this campaign will serve to separate the sheep from the goats."

There was prolonged applause after these remarks.

Following Simmons' speech, Bilheimer introduced the Red Cross officials on the speakers' platform to the audience. He did it in his inimitable way, which greatly amused the audience.

Those introduced were: Mrs. Frank V. Hammar, Melville L. Wilkinson, Walker Hill, Festus J. Wade and J. L. Johnston. After each introduction Bilheimer would shout "Give 'em a welcome, boys," and cheering would follow.

St. Louis a Red Cross Knight.

Archbishop John J. Glennon, the next speaker, said that the Red Cross symbolized bleeding humanity. Holding up one of the symbols, he said:

"Men and women of St. Louis, the symbol of the cross of red stands for bleeding humanity that appeals to you for help. St. Louis, for whom this city was named, was a Red Cross knight. He died in an attempt to rescue the tomb of our Savior, and the tomb that he failed to rescue is today rescued by the armies of the allies."

Closing, the archbishop said he wanted to announce that the Knights of Columbus of St. Louis, who have sent 1000 of their 4000 members to the war, were ready to subscribe immediately for 2500 memberships.

Lee Meriwether, who returned several months ago from a diplomatic mission abroad, told about Prussianism and described Red Cross work he had seen on the French and Italian front.

"The German people for 40 years have let out their thinking as we let out our laundry. They have let out their government to one man, who calls himself kaiser and claims partnership with God. This kaiser has deluded them and is deluding them still. Now, I wish the people of Germany could see this

great assemblage and hear its voice against autocracy. They would realize then that though Americans love peace they love liberty more."

Audience Cheers for Wilson.

Meriwether said the Red Cross was an emblem which meant love and sacrifice and devotion.

Dr. Z. B. T. Phillips, the next speaker, brought to the chairman's attention the fact that there had been no cheering for President Wilson, and Bilheimer jumped to his feet and began leading the audience in cheers for the president. Dr. Phillips made an appeal for Red Cross membership.

Between the speeches the Boy Scouts canvassed the audience for memberships and the audience sang patriotic songs, led by Johnny Adams and Alfred E. Buss.

The enrollment stage of the Red Cross Christmas membership campaign has been reached, and henceforth until the evening of December 24 an army of thousands of men and women will devote its energies to the task of rolling up a roster of 500,000 in the St. Louis district, embracing this city, East St. Louis and St. Louis County.

Precincts to Have Booths.

In St. Louis, at 9 o'clock this morning, each of the 500 precincts will have a booth open for registrants. Similar arrangements will prevail in the city east of the river, and in the county preparations have been made for the convenient registration of every citizen who feels that the call of his or her country to a patriotic service is compellingly sacred.

Not less than 1000 women will be in attendance at the St. Louis booths daily, and heavy re-enforcements of men for work in each of the precincts have been organized. The workers were surrendered to the cause by employers, while the women enlistments are from the ranks of the Women's Committee of the Council of National Defense and clubs generally which responded to the appeal of that organization for co-operation.

In response to a call sent out Saturday by Mayor Kiel and Commissioners Talbert and Schmoll of the municipal staff, 500 men active in politics in every precinct of the city assembled at the City Hall yesterday morning to enlist in the Red Cross membership drive. The mayor presided at the conference, and the outcome was a compact organization that will be in the crusade until the close, with all the individual enthusiasm possible. These workers will be utilized in their respective precincts, where they know and are known by nearly every resident.

It was suggested with emphasis by the Campaign Executive Committee that in the house-to-house canvass that is to be made in behalf of the Red Cross, the men engaged in it should be held distinct from the petty canvassers who annoy the average householder. The service in this instance is peculiarly national and of a war nature, and not only should it be recognized with uniform courtesy, but those to whom they bring the call for enlistment are expected to give it favorable consideration with promptness that delay may be avoided.

Slurring Remarks to Be Reported.

In this connection it was stated by Chairman Harry F. Knight that the committee had been officially admonished to have the canvassers and other workers report every instance of slurring remarks concerning the war undertaking of the nation in any of its details. Information of this nature reaching the committee will be at once submitted to the proper federal authorities.

< *St. Louis Globe-Democrat* newspaper clipping titled "8000 Pack Coliseum in Drive to Get 10,000,000 New Red Cross Members," December 1917
Missouri Historical Society Collections
A0258-00006

⋀ Barrel for collecting fruit pits and nut shells for use in gas mask filters, ca. 1918
Missouri Historical Society Collections
P0821-01-153

˅ Red Cross knit scarf and mittens, ca. 1917
Missouri Historical Society Collections
2005-079-0003

The United States needs your help to protect the lives of our soldiers.
———
Read this Card carefully
———
Talk to your friends about this

˄ Red Cross knitting needles, ca. 1918
Missouri Historical Society Collections
X14919

< > Red Cross card requesting fruit pits and nut shells for use in gas mask filters, ca. 1917
Missouri Historical Society Collections
A1771-00004

⌃ Red Cross knitting drive, ca. 1918
Missouri Historical Society Collections
P0229-02002

➤ Red Cross nurse's aide uniform of Anne Kennett Farrar, ca. 1917
Missouri Historical Society Collections
1977-086-0023

PIN THIS ON YOUR KITCHEN DOOR

Help Save a Soldier's Life

In order to make the most efficient carbon for gas masks, to save our men from the horrible death caused by German poison gas, our Government is in dire need of great quantities of the following materials:

PEACH STONES	APRICOT PITS
PRUNE PITS	PLUM PITS
OLIVE PITS	DATE SEEDS
CHERRY PITS	BUTTER-NUT SHELLS
WALNUT SHELLS	BRAZIL NUT SHELLS
HICKORY-NUT SHELLS	

Collect all you can of these materials, dry them thoroughly and deliver at least once each month to any branch post-office or deposit in barrels placed in front of public schools and in department stores. Small neatly prepared packages may be delivered to letter carriers. Large packages should be delivered to the warehouse at 110 N. 8th Street between 10 A. M. and 12 noon and 2 and 4 P. M.

ST. LOUIS CHAPTER
AMERICAN RED CROSS.

ST. LOUIS CHAPTER
AMERICAN RED CROSS

S. W. Cor. 9th and Olive

Directions for Knitting

REVERSIBLE WRISTLETS

4 Red Cross Needles No. 1.

Cast 52 stitches on 3 needles: 16-16-20.
Knit 2, purl 2, for 3 inches.

THUMB OPENING No. 1:

Knit 2, purl 2, to end of third needle. Turn. Knit and purl to the end of first needle, always slipping first stitch. Turn. Continue to knit back and forth for 2 inches.

Then knit 2, purl 2, all the way around for 3 inches.

THUMB OPENING No. 2:

Make a second thumb opening like thumb opening No. 1. Then knit 2, purl 2 all the way around for 3 inches. Bind off loosely. Buttonhole thumb openings.

MUFFLER

3 Hanks of Yarn (¾ lb.); 1 pair Red Cross needles No. 3.

Cast on 50 stitches or 11 inches. Plain knitting for 72 inches.

HELMET

5 Red Cross Needles No. 2.

TOP:

Cast on 20 stitches. Knit plain 28 ridges (always slipping first stitch). On the last row, throw in 4 extra stitches.

With 2nd needle pick up 28 stitches on side of crown.

With 3rd needle pick up 20 stitches at end of crown.

With 4th needle pick up 28 stitches on other side of crown.

There are now 100 stitches: 24 on 1st needle; 28 on 2nd needle; 20 on 3rd needle; 28 on 4th needle.

Knit 2, purl 2, for 4½ inches. On the last round, bind off the last 2 stitches of the second needle, the 20 stitches of the third needle and the first 2 stitches of the fourth needle for the face opening.

Knit 2, purl 2, back and forth for 2 inches, always knitting or purling the first stitch.

Cast on 24 stitches, and divide stitches on the four needles as before. Knit 2, purl 2, for 6 inches.

FRONT CAPE:

On the last round, knit (do not purl the capes) the last 13 stitches on the fourth needle, the 24 stitches on the first needle and 13 stitches on the second needle onto a No. 2 needle. You now have 50 stitches on this needle. Knit 36 ridges. Bind off.

BACK CAPE:

Slip the remaining 50 stitches onto the No. 2 needle. Knit 36 ridges. Bind off.

Do not sew edges of capes together.

SLEEVELESS SWEATER

2 Red Cross Needles No. 3.

Cast on 80 stitches. Knit 2, purl 2 stitches for 4 inches. Knit plain until sweater measures 23 inches. Knit 28 stitches, bind off loosely 24 stitches for neck. Knit 28 stitches. Knit 7 ridges on each shoulder, cast on 24 stitches. Knit plain for 19 inches. Purl 2, knit 2 for 4 inches. Sew up sides, leaving 9 inches for armholes. 2 rows single crochet around neck and 1 row single crochet around armholes.

For heavy yarn, cast on 72 stitches, binding off loosely 20 stitches for neck, leaving 26 stitches for each shoulder.

⌃ **Directions for knitting issued by the St. Louis chapter of the American Red Cross, ca. 1917**
Missouri Historical Society Collections
A1771-00005

➤ **Paper poster displayed in windows to show American Red Cross membership, ca. 1917**
Missouri Historical Society Collections
A1771-00003

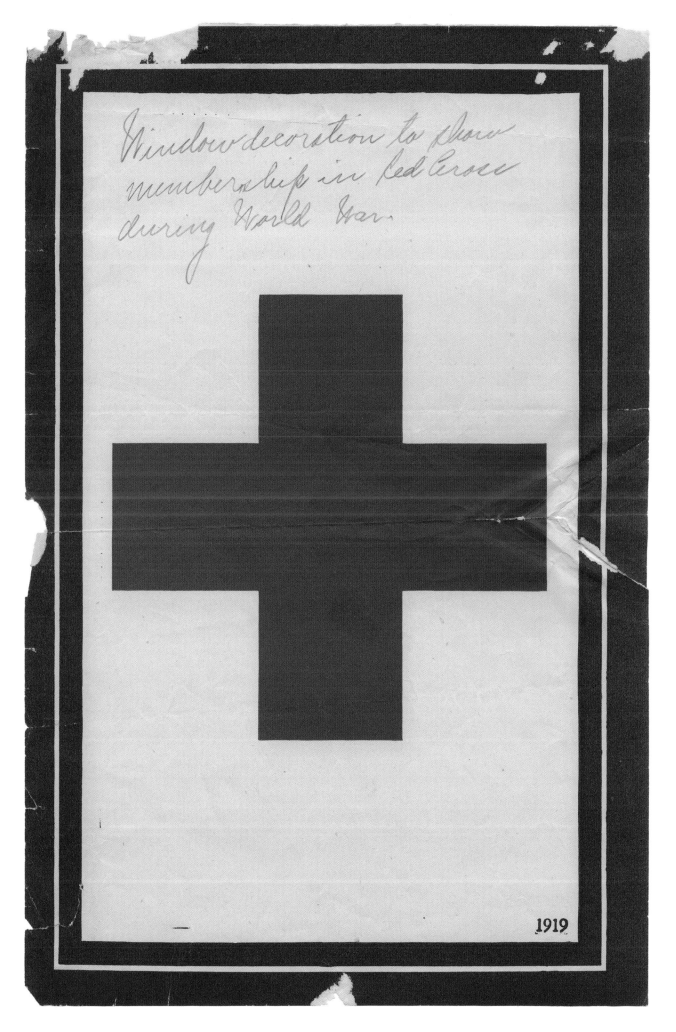

Window decoration to show membership in Red Cross during World War.

1919

1918 INFLUENZA EPIDEMIC

Not every World War I battle was fought with a gun. The 1918 influenza epidemic was one of the worst in world history. The flu infected an estimated 500 million people worldwide, killing between 50 and 100 million. The war accelerated the spread of the virus as millions of people moved across the globe and concentrated in Europe. Unlike typical flu outbreaks, Spanish influenza predominantly killed healthy young adults rather than the elderly, sick, and children.

The earliest reports of Spanish influenza in the United States came from Camp Funston, Kansas, in March 1918. Local cases of the flu first appeared at Jefferson Barracks seven months later.

St. Louis members of the Red Cross Motor Ambulance Corps removing influenza sufferer from home at Etzel and Page avenues.

‹ **Workers from the St. Louis chapter of the American Red Cross collecting victims of the flu epidemic, 1918**
St. Louis Post-Dispatch

MAX C. STARKLOFF, M. D.,
PHYSICIAN & SURGEON,
HEALTH COMMISSIONER.

⌃ **Dr. Max C. Starkloff, ca. 1900**
Missouri Historical Society Collections
N13359

› **St. Louis Chamber of Commerce letter regarding the flu epidemic, October 1918**
Missouri Historical Society Collections
A0129-00049

DR. MAX C. STARKLOFF SPARES ST. LOUIS

Under the leadership of Health Commissioner Dr. Max C. Starkloff, St. Louis reacted quickly and effectively to Spanish influenza. When the virus was first reported in the United States, Starkloff began monitoring local military installations. As soon as cases appeared at Jefferson Barracks in early October 1918, Starkloff met with St. Louis mayor Henry Kiel to discuss the city's plan.

The men agreed to institute a ban on public gatherings, which involved closing churches, theaters, pool halls, and other public venues. The ban lasted from October 8 until December 28. As a result, St. Louis experienced far lower death rates from Spanish influenza than other major American cities.

ST. LOUIS CHAMBER OF COMMERCE

510 LOCUST STREET

JACKSON JOHNSON, President
GEORGE D. MARKHAM, First Vice-President
VINCENT L. PRICE, Second Vice-President
L. WADE CHILDRESS, Third Vice-President
J. A. LEWIS, Treasurer
PAUL V. BUNN, General Secretary

PHONES {MAIN 4620
{CENTRAL 7565

 St. Louis, Mo.,

October 8, 1918.

Gentlemen:

Influenza conditions in St. Louis have suddenly reached a serious stage. A conference of prominent medical men and Red Cross officials, at which the Chamber of Commerce was also represented, was held Monday morning, and it was decided to close public schools, theatres, picture shows and other places where people congregate.

The Health Commissioner has been given absolute authority by a proclamation of the Mayor, to close all places he may deem necessary. It is only a short step from the closing of these places, to the closing of the factories. For that reason we are bringing the situation immediately to your attention, because we feel that by proper precaution now the necessity of this might be eliminated.

At the conference it was decided if the business institutions carry out every precaution they would be able to remain open unless the disease became prevalent in any one factory or any one district. In case the Health Commissioner finds influenza in a factory, he has the power to close that plant, even if it were making war material. We would suggest that you rush your production as fast as possible, and THAT YOU SEND HOME EVERY CASE OF COLD OR "SNIFFLES" among your employees, telling them to go to bed, keep warm, get on a light diet, send for a physician in preference to doctoring themselves, as this disease spreads very rapidly.

The best preventative recommended by the medical profession in general, is fresh air and sunshine, being careful of the food that is eaten, plenty of rest, not to get the feet wet. In fact, to take especially good care of one's self. For further information we are enclosing a bulletin issued by the American Red Cross.

The fact that St. Louis has not suffered in a greater measure from the epidemic is due, no doubt, to the unusually favorable climatic conditions in the last few days. The epidemic will probably increase in the next week or two, especially if there is a change to cooler weather with rain.

We feel that if each business concern and factory in St. Louis exercises unusual vigilance in this respect, that it will not be necessary, so far as we can be seen now, to curtail general business or industrial production.

Very truly yours,

P. V. Bunn

WBW:AK.

General Secretary.

P. S. While this applies especially to factories, we are sending it to our entire membership, asking them to use every means possible to curtail the spread of Influenza.

JAMES MONTGOMERY FLAGG

THE Y. M. C. A. Hut is home to-day for two million boys over there, and for another million on this side. Your money helped to build the Huts; and is helping to keep them the bright spot in the soldiers' and sailors' lives.

Follow your money through the pages of this book, and see how many different good things it is doing for our boys.

SUPPORTING TROOPS ON THE HOME FRONT

Across St. Louis, organizations raised money to support troops at home and overseas. These groups provided refreshment, religious services, and entertainment to soldiers traveling through the city. They also raised funds in support of their work in Europe.

Early in the war, the major auxiliary organizations involved in war service devised a plan by which American soldiers from the three major faiths at the time were ministered to separately. Protestants were ministered to by the YMCA, Catholics by the Knights of Columbus, and Jews by the Jewish Welfare Board.

◄ **Pamphlet explaining the YMCA's role in World War I, ca. 1918**
Missouri Historical Society Collections
A1771-00019

∧ **Knights of Columbus poster, 1917**
Library of Congress
LC-USZC4-10131

◄ **Jewish Welfare Board poster, 1918**
Library of Congress
LC-DIG-ppmsca-05652

∨ **YMCA National War Work Council pennant, ca. 1918**
Missouri Historical Society Collections
X14918

Name a Tank Contest

These contests give every county an opportunity to compete on a fair basis; they also enable each town and city to compete with only those cities in the same class.

Illustrated bulletins showing the progress of each contest will be issued as frequently as possible, probably daily, so that each county may know just how it stands with other counties.

The "Over the Top" contest in the Third Campaign caused a good deal of interest, but it also caused some dissatisfaction on the part of a few counties. This dissatisfaction was almost invariably due to the fact that the counties had not turned in their reports promptly.

The same situation will exist in these contests unless the counties and cities contesting get in their reports promptly and in the proper form. If any county or city does not show up well, the fault must rest with the county or city because the bulletins will be based each day on the very latest reports received up to the hour of closing.

It will take one day to get these bulletins out and one day to print them; therefore when the information gets to the different counties it will be two or three days old. However, every county will be on an equal basis and, therefore, each county will know how it stands relatively to the other counties.

In order to make these contests interesting, we expect to follow the plan adopted in "Over the Top" contest in the Third Campaign. We will good naturedly roast some counties and pat others on the back, according to the returns which we receive. Please understand that this is all good natured and is merely intended to arouse feelings of rivalry and spur each con-

testant on to greater efforts. Remember, also, that we are all working in a good cause and that we might as well have a little fun as we go along.

In getting in your reports, please note that reports are required on two things—one is amount of subscriptions and the other is number of subscriptions. Unless both reports are sent in at the same time, and promptly, a county may show up well on the tank contest and poorly on the ship contest.

Let's enter this contest in the proper spirit and not only show the other counties in each State what you can do, but by united effort let's show the entire country what the Eighth District can do. We did it before—we can do it again.

V. L. PRICE,
General Director of Sales.

H. S. GARDNER.
Director of Publicity.

FUNDING THE WAR

The Great War cost the United States more than $22 billion. Instead of funding the nation's war involvement through taxation, President Woodrow Wilson relied on bonds and government loans to provide the necessary capital. The resulting effort to raise funds involved a vast promotional campaign led by the Committee on Public Information.

⌃ **Explanation of the Eighth Federal Reserve District's "Name a Tank" contest, 1918**
Missouri Historical Society Collections
A1771-00011

◄ **War Savings Service arm tag, ca. 1918**
Missouri Historical Society Collections
X13615

▼ **Pamphlet explaining liberty bonds and their use, 1918**
Missouri Historical Society Collections
A1771-00012

WHAT YOUR MONEY BUYS

Don't let the SON go down

Buy 4th Liberty BONDS

OWN THE HUN
WITH DOLLAR AND GUN

P-31

◄ **War Savings Service pin, ca. 1918**
Missouri Historical Society Collections
X09934

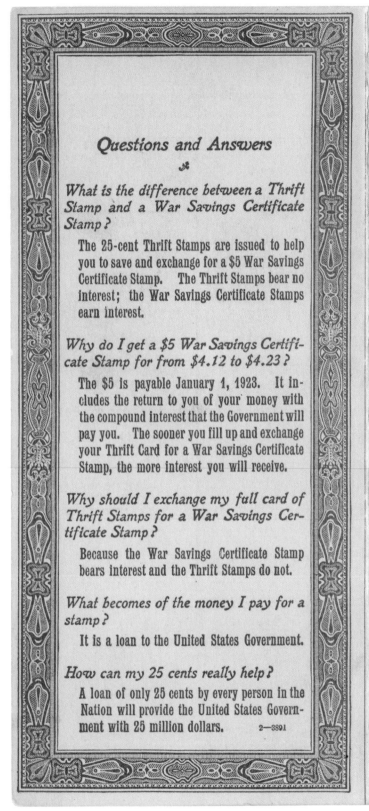

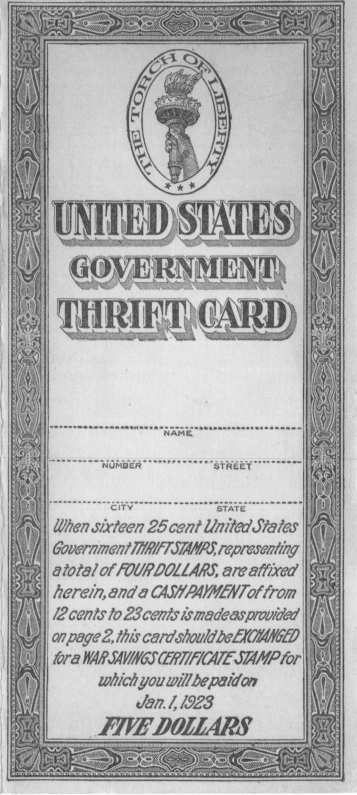

Questions and Answers

What is the difference between a Thrift Stamp and a War Savings Certificate Stamp?

The 25-cent Thrift Stamps are issued to help you to save and exchange for a $5 War Savings Certificate Stamp. The Thrift Stamps bear no interest; the War Savings Certificate Stamps earn interest.

Why do I get a $5 War Savings Certificate Stamp for from $4.12 to $4.23?

The $5 is payable January 1, 1923. It includes the return to you of your money with the compound interest that the Government will pay you. The sooner you fill up and exchange your Thrift Card for a War Savings Certificate Stamp, the more interest you will receive.

Why should I exchange my full card of Thrift Stamps for a War Savings Certificate Stamp?

Because the War Savings Certificate Stamp bears interest and the Thrift Stamps do not.

What becomes of the money I pay for a stamp?

It is a loan to the United States Government.

How can my 25 cents really help?

A loan of only 25 cents by every person in the Nation will provide the United States Government with 25 million dollars.

2—3891

THE TORCH OF LIBERTY

UNITED STATES GOVERNMENT THRIFT CARD

NAME

NUMBER   STREET

CITY   STATE

When sixteen 25 cent United States Government THRIFT STAMPS, representing a total of FOUR DOLLARS, are affixed herein, and a CASH PAYMENT of from 12 cents to 23 cents is made as provided on page 2, this card should be EXCHANGED for a WAR SAVINGS CERTIFICATE STAMP for which you will be paid on Jan. 1, 1923

FIVE DOLLARS

∧ **War Savings Service card with thrift stamps, ca. 1918**
Missouri Historical Society Collections
A1771-00010

▲ **First Liberty Loan pin, 1917**
Missouri Historical Society Collections
1998-155-0002

◄ **Second Liberty Loan pin, 1917**
Missouri Historical Society Collections
X09924

▼ **Third Liberty Loan pin, 1918**
Missouri Historical Society Collections
1994-085-0113

To The Federal Reserve Bank of St. Louis
Fiscal Agent of the United States

STATEMENT OF
Third Liberty Loan Subscriptions

Handled by

I.

(A) This Bank received subscriptions for Third Liberty Loan Bonds from............... subscribers

amounting in the aggregate to.. $..............................

(B) This bank purchased for its own investment, Third Liberty Loan Bonds amounting to........ $..............................

Total amount of Third Liberty Loan Bonds which this bank subscribed for account of

itself and subscribers... $..............................

NOTE: In paragraph (A) we include all full paid subscriptions, all subscriptions received on the Government payment plan and all subscriptions received on any special installment plan. Where corporations or employers placed subscriptions with us and resold bonds to employees, we ascertained the number of sales by such corporation or employer and included the number of purchasers in the above total subscriptions.

II.

This Bank subscribed through the Federal Reserve Bank of St. Louis for Third Liberty Loan

Bonds aggregating .... $..............................

III.

This Bank filed subscriptions with other incorporated Banks or Trust Companies and desires credit for same to the extent of $.., as shown by schedule on reverse.

IV.

The subscriptions which this Bank filed with the Federal Reserve Bank of St. Louis included subscriptions of other Banks amounting to $................................. Please give credit according to schedule on reverse.

V.

At the present time this Bank owns outright First Liberty Loan 3½% or converted 4% Bonds

amounting to .... $..............................

This does not include any bonds which we are carrying for customers.

VI.

At the present time this Bank owns Second Liberty Loan 4% Bonds amounting to $..............................
This does not include any bonds which we are carrying for customers.

....
Signature of Bank Officer.

....
Title

Date..

⌃ Fourth Liberty Loan banner, 1918
Missouri Historical Society Collections
1922-043-0001

➤ Fourth Liberty Loan pin, 1918
Missouri Historical Society Collections
1994-085-0112

◄ Blank form for a Third Liberty Loan subscription, 1918
Missouri Historical Society Collections
A1771-00021

Comic touting St. Louis as first district to sell its quota of victory loans, ca. 1919

Missouri Historical Society Collections
A1771-00015

⌃ Fifth Victory Liberty Loan pin, 1919
Missouri Historical Society Collections
1926-017-0004

❯ Fifth Victory Liberty Loan flyer dropped from airplanes over St. Louis, ca. 1919
Missouri Historical Society Collections
P0155-00132_0001, P0155-00132_0002

⌄ Fifth Victory Liberty Loan medal made from captured German artillery, 1919
Missouri Historical Society Collections
1992-021-0001

SERVICE FLAGS

St. Louisans took great pride in their loved ones' military service, pride that was visible throughout the city in the form of service flags that hung in windows, on church rafters, and in public buildings. Also known as "son in service flags" or "blue star flags," service flags originated during World War I as a way to publicly share that members of one's family were serving in the military. Each blue star on a flag represented an individual serving.

Many St. Louis families had flags bearing three or more stars for each of their relatives in the war. Today, service flags can still be seen on display citywide.

GOLD STARS

When a loved one made the ultimate sacrifice, it became customary to cover the blue star on the service flag with gold. Organizations such as the Gold Star Mothers and Gold Star Families took their names from this practice of honoring those who gave their lives in military service.

∧ **Service flag of Pvt. William Preetorius, 128th Field Artillery, ca. 1918**
Missouri Historical Society Collections
1926-048-0004

∧ **Markham Presbyterian Church service banner, ca. 1918**
Missouri Historical Society Collections
1940-017-0001

❯ **Company G, 1st Regiment, Missouri Home Guard service banner, ca. 1918**
Missouri Historical Society Collections
1919-070-0002

VICTORY AND HOMECOMING

After years of brutal fighting, armistice was officially declared in November 1918. St. Louis newspaper headlines trumpeted the war's end, and people poured into the streets as celebrations broke out downtown. The festivities continued into the summer of 1919 when the last Missouri soldiers returned home and paraded through the streets of St. Louis. Meanwhile, the work of rebuilding began as world leaders gathered at Versailles, France, to initiate negotiation of a peace treaty.

ARMISTICE IS DECLARED ON NOVEMBER 11, 1918

The success of the Meuse-Argonne Offensive pressed Germany to seek an end to the fighting. Aboard a railcar 37 miles north of Paris, Allied and German delegations signed an armistice that declared a cessation of hostilities effective at the 11th hour of the 11th day of the 11th month in 1918. It would be another six months before the signing of an official treaty ending the war.

^ Peace rattle used in St. Louis to celebrate the end of World War I, ca. 1918
Missouri Historical Society Collections
2008-073-0008

^ Armistice Day celebrations on Olive St., November 1918
Missouri Historical Society Collections
P0821-01-178

WILSON'S 14 POINTS, JANUARY 1918

President Wilson intended to be a significant player during the peace negotiations, and he secured that role thanks to America's part in the Allied victory.

Nearly a year before the cessation of hostilities on the Western Front, on January 8, 1918, Wilson issued a 14-point blueprint for achieving and maintaining peace. His plan called for diplomatic transparency, freedom of the seas, equality of trade, restoration of occupied territories, and the forming of a League of Nations. It was on the basis of these points that Germany wished to begin the process of negotiating the armistice and peace.

◄ *St. Louis Post-Dispatch* front page from January 8, 1918
Missouri Historical Society Collections
GRA00229

▼ Newspaper clipping titled "President Announces Terms of Armistice," November 11, 1918
St. Louis Post-Dispatch

THE PARIS PEACE CONFERENCE AND THE TREATY OF VERSAILLES, 1919

In January 1919 the leaders of the Allied nations of France, Great Britain, Italy, and the United States began negotiating an official peace treaty. Germany was excluded from the discussions until May, when its leaders were presented with a draft of the Treaty of Versailles.

Germany had hoped President Wilson's 14 points would be the guiding principles of the treaty, but it soon discovered that Great Britain and France had taken the document in a different direction. Seeking to punish

CONGRESS REJECTS THE TREATY OF VERSAILLES

"What is it that they want us in for? Why, they want us in for the same reason that they want us to cancel their debts to us. They want us to bear the expense. They want us in to guarantee that whenever they get a majority in the League that wants to do something, the tremendous force of the United States will be there to help accomplish it."—Senator James Reed of Missouri, speaking against the League of Nations on March 2, 1921

When he returned to US soil, President Wilson had high hopes for obtaining congressional approval for the Treaty of Versailles and establishing the League of Nations, an international organization founded to maintain world peace. Yet he faced a Republican-majority Congress and a group of 12 to 18 Republican and Democrat senators—the so-called Irreconcilables—who staunchly opposed ratification. Wilson also alienated much of his progressive base with his wartime domestic policies, leading to half-hearted support from his own party. Ultimately the US neither ratified the Treaty of Versailles nor entered the League of Nations.

◀ **Crowded hall at the Palace of Versailles during signing of the peace treaty, June 1919**
Library of Congress
LC-USZ62-392

Germany, Great Britain and France had helped draft a treaty that required Germany to pay reparations to the Allied countries, surrender overseas territory, decrease its military, and accept exclusive blame for the war. Wilson had objected to this approach but ultimately accepted the proposed terms in exchange for a provision to establish the League of Nations.

The Treaty of Versailles was signed on June 28, 1919—exactly five years after the assassination of Archduke Franz Ferdinand, the incident that sparked the conflict.

HOMECOMING IN ST. LOUIS

Through the spring and summer of 1919, St. Louis hosted grand parades for returning troops. The parade given for St. Louis's 138th Infantry Regiment began at Union Blvd. near Forest Park and stretched six miles to St. Louis City Hall, near where the Soldiers Memorial Military Museum is located today.

The *St. Louis Post-Dispatch* had this to say of the parade: "Possibly half a million people saw the hardened men swing by in platoon formation, with combat packs, steel helmets and fixed bayonets. Probably no Veiled Prophet parade was seen by more people."

➤ **Homecoming parade for the 128th Field Artillery, 1919**
Missouri Historical Society Collections
P0456-00003

⌃ **Homecoming parade for St. Louis's World War I soldiers, 1919**
Missouri Historical Society Collections
P0456-00006

⌃ **89th Division passing through the Court of Honor, 1919**
Missouri Historical Society Collections
P0821-01-304

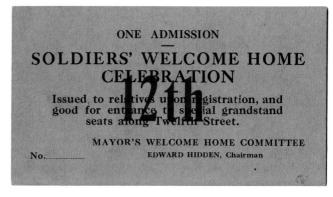

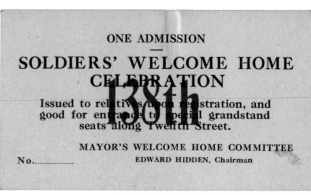

> Members of the 12th Engineers receiving medals, 1919
Missouri Historical Society Collections
P0234-00058

ⱽ Ticket to attend the 12th Engineers' homecoming celebration, 1919
Missouri Historical Society Collections
A1771-00009

⌃ Ticket to attend the 138th Infantry Regiment's homecoming celebration, 1919
Missouri Historical Society Collections
A1771-00008

◄ Fighting 89th homecoming pennant, 1919
Missouri Historical Society Collections
1939-028-0001

> Commemorative lighter gifted by the City of St. Louis to members of the 35th Infantry Division, 1919
Missouri Historical Society Collections
X13613

PART 4
ST. LOUIS HONORS AND REMEMBERS

"We in America do not build monuments to war; we do not build monuments to conquests; we build monuments to commemorate the spirit of sacrifice in war—reminders of our desire for peace."
—President Franklin Roosevelt, speaking at the dedication of the Soldiers Memorial site on October 14, 1936

IN THE YEARS FOLLOWING WORLD WAR I, ST. LOUIS AND THE nation sought to honor those who made the ultimate sacrifice and care for the millions of servicemen who returned home.

Commemorative monuments and memorials were raised across the city during the 1920s and 1930s. At the same time, dozens of St. Louis mothers and widows traveled to France to visit the battlefields where their loved ones were buried.

Veterans returning to St. Louis sought to maintain bonds forged on the battlefields of Europe by organizing groups to petition for veterans' rights and benefits. The largest of these, the American Legion, held its first domestic caucus in St. Louis in May 1919, forever cementing the city as its birthplace.

*Women's Overse
Th
June 16th*

ervice League Banquet
ake
Chicago

**⌃ Women's Overseas Service League
banquet in Chicago, 1923**
*Courtesy of the National World War I Museum and Memorial,
Kansas City, Missouri, U.S.A.*
1980.19.24

MEMORIALIZATION

Of the more than 156,000 Missourians who served in the armed forces; worked as nurses; or volunteered with the YMCA, Red Cross, and other war-service organizations, nearly 3,500 lost their lives, including 1,075 St. Louisans. Across the state and overseas, monuments were raised to honor the service and sacrifice of these brave individuals. A statewide effort to document the stories of the Great War's participants began simultaneously.

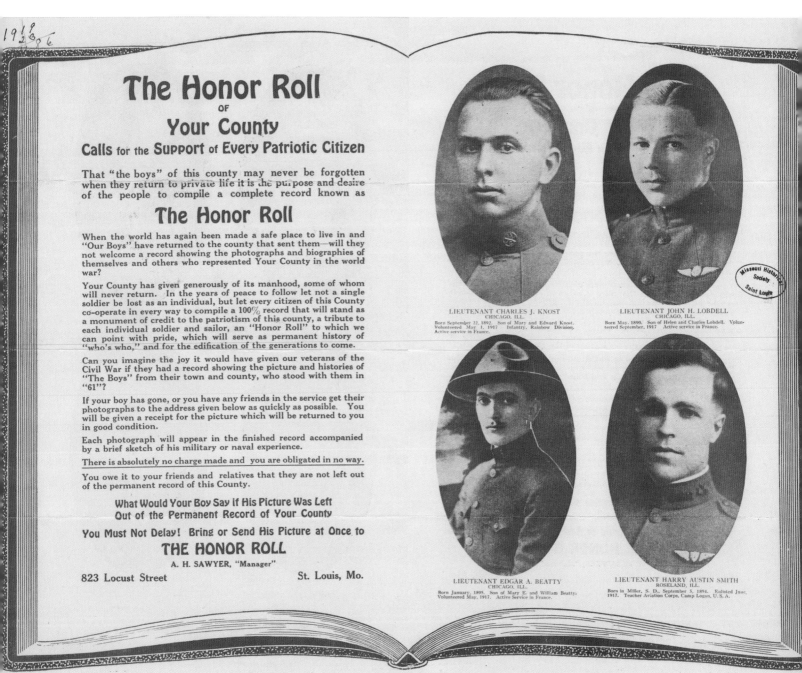

⌃ **Flyer requesting citizens of St. Louis City and County to share information about their military service, ca. 1920**
Missouri Historical Society Collections
A1771-00018

MISSOURI SOLDIERS' RECORDS AND MISSOURI SERVICE MEDALS

The State of Missouri sought to commemorate Missouri veterans by gathering the details of their service and publishing a collection of this information by county, to be issued to each Missourian based on county of residence. Veterans received a Missouri Service Medal as an incentive to provide their records. The Missouri Historical Society was one of the leading organizations collecting this information from veterans in St. Louis and St. Louis County.

> WWI Missouri Service Medal of Cpt. Arthur Proetz, ca. 1920
Missouri Historical Society Collections
1968-042-0005

A MONUMENT TO MISSOURI SOLDIERS IN FRANCE

Sculpted by St. Louisan Nancy Coonsman Hahn and erected by the State of Missouri in 1922, the Missouri First World War Monument near Cheppy, France, was dedicated to those Missourians who gave their lives during the Great War. The monument includes a raised stone pedestal surmounted by the Angel of Victory in bronze.

12TH ENGINEERS MONUMENT

At a 12th Engineers' reunion held on June 25, 1922, a monument was unveiled on the banks of the Mississippi River at the Chain of Rocks, near where the regiment had trained five years earlier. The monument was a red granite pyramid marked with a bronze tablet. It was designed and erected by members of the 12th Engineers to honor those who had lost their lives during the war. The monument has since been taken down—all that remains is this bronze plaque.

> Bronze plaque from the 12th Engineers Monument, ca. 1922
Soldiers Memorial Military Museum Collections
SMX03847

SOLDIERS MEMORIAL MILITARY MUSEUM

The Soldiers Memorial Military Museum was built as a memorial to honor the 1,075 St. Louisans who made the ultimate sacrifice during the War to End All Wars. Development began in 1925 with the formation of a Memorial Plaza Commission that supervised the creation of the Memorial Plaza and Soldiers Memorial. Designed by St. Louis architecture firm Mauran, Russell & Crowell, the Soldiers Memorial building features statues entitled *Courage*, *Loyalty*, *Sacrifice*, and *Vision* created by St. Louis–born sculptor Walker Hancock.

Soldiers Memorial first opened on Memorial Day 1938 and quickly became a center for veterans' activities in the city.

◀ **Soldiers Memorial postcard, ca. 1940**
Missouri Historical Society Collections
P0363-00072

▼ **President Franklin Roosevelt dedicating the Soldiers Memorial site, 1936**
Missouri Historical Society Collections
P0403-P00001N

VETERANS' ORGANIZATIONS

Following the war, the US had more military veterans than ever before. In response, Congress established a new system for veterans' benefits, laying the groundwork for many of the veterans' programs still in place today. These programs included compensation for disabled veterans, insurance, and job assistance.

The large number of veterans who returned home to St. Louis ensured the city would play an integral role in the foundation of one of the largest veterans' organizations—the American Legion—in the years following the war.

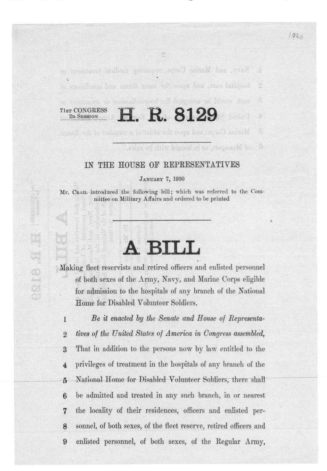

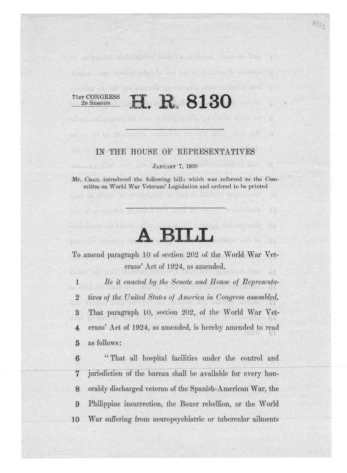

CARING FOR VETERANS

In 1921, Congress created the Veterans Bureau—the predecessor of today's US Department of Veterans Affairs. The Veterans Bureau oversaw veterans' benefits and established hospitals for veterans.

The original portion of the VA Medical Center at Jefferson Barracks was built by the Veterans Bureau in 1923 to provide care to veterans in St. Louis and the surrounding region. The hospital still operates today as part of the larger regional VA system.

∧ ＞ Three congressional bills regarding benefits for World War I veterans, 1930–1931
Missouri Historical Society Collections
A0475-00003, A0475-00004, A0475-00005

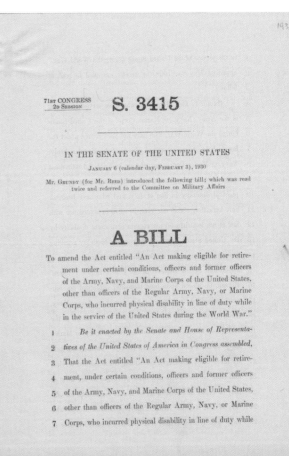

> **Fund for Disabled American Veterans of the World War ribbon, ca. 1920**
Missouri Historical Society Collections
A1061

˅ **Application for compensation of disabled World War I veterans, 1927**
Missouri Historical Society Collections
A0475

> ***Where Do We Go From Here?* booklet of John Counts, ca. 1920**
Missouri Historical Society Collections
2007-056-0006

DEPARTMENT OF LABOR
U. S. EMPLOYMENT SERVICE   (In

EMPLOYMENT BUREAU
SOLDIERS, SAILORS AND MARINES
902 OLIVE STREET, ST. LOUIS
                                            December 30, 1918.

Henze's Old Rock Bakery Co.
St. Louis.

Gentlemen:-

      The United States Department of Labor has established an Employment Bureau for Soldiers, Sailors & Marines at 902 Olive street, St. Louis, for the purpose of securing employment for the thousands of young men returning from the camps and over-seas.

      Hundreds apply to us every day for something to do, but as we have so many more applicants than positions, we are obliged to turn many away.

      Our great difficulty is in finding places for them.

      Therefore, in order to let the general public know that our office has been established, and that we have a long waiting list of Soldiers and Sailors anxious to go to work, we are going to advertise the fact by placing an advertisement in every street car in St. Louis, and nearby towns, which we feel will reach just the persons who are in position to help us.

      As the Government does not make an allowance for advertising, it becomes necessary to ask a number of firms and individuals to help bear the expense of this patriotic service.

      Will you therefore be one to donate $25. for the purpose? All details have been arranged with the Advertising Co. You need only to mail your check for $25. payable to the St. Louis Union Bank, in enclosed envelope which does not need a stamp, and send the blank below with it.

      Each advertisement covered by your contribution will have a notice with your name and address printed thereon, reading about as follows-

      "This space donated by Henze's Old Rock Bakery Co."

      We will mail you a few of the cards bearing your name, which should be placed in prominent places, so that as much publicity as possible may be given to our work.

      May we ask for immediate and favorable consideration of this request?

               Yours very truly,

                    A. H. Brown

                    Federal Director,
                    U.S.Employment Service
                    State of Missouri

- -

      Tear off here and mail in enclosed envelope with your check.

      Enclosed is check for $25. for advertising the Employment Bureau for Soldiers, Sailors & Marines in the Street cars of St. Louis, and nearby towns. The name written on last line is to appear on the advertisement.

              Sign here- - - - - - - - - - - - - - - - - - - -
      Write here how you wish name to be printed on the advertisement.

- -

∧ ≻ Forty & Eight smock and cap of Musician Samuel Frank, 1950–2005
Missouri Historical Society Collections
2007-061-0001, 2007-061-0002

AMERICAN LEGION AND THE FORTY & EIGHT

The largest postwar veterans' organization was the American Legion. The group held its first domestic caucus—and adopted its official constitution, which described its purpose and organization—in St. Louis in May 1919 at the Shubert Theatre on Tucker Blvd. and Olive St. The American Legion was formally established later that year, and St. Louis is still recognized as its birthplace.

American Legion leaders later founded an honor society called the La Société des Quarante Hommes et Huit Chevaux, or the Society of Forty Men and Eight Horses. The name references the boxcars used to transport troops in France that were marked "40/8," indicating the car could hold 40 men or 8 horses.

≻ Medal commemorating the founding of the American Legion, ca. 1935
Missouri Historical Society Collections
1935-015-0003

≺ US Department of Labor letter about hiring veterans, ca. 1920
Missouri Historical Society Collections
A0686

CONSTITUTION
AMERICAN LEGION
As adopted by the St. Louis Caucus, May 10th, 1919

PREAMBLE

For God and country we associate ourselves together for the following purposes:

To uphold and defend the Constitution of the United States of America; to maintain law and order; to foster and perpetuate a one hundred percent Americanism; to preserve the memories and incidents of our association in the Great War; to inculcate a sense of individual obligation to the community, state and nation; to combat the autocracy of both the classes and the masses; to make right the master of might; to promote peace and good will on earth; to safeguard and transmit to posterity the principles of justice, freedom and democracy; to consecrate and sanctify our comradship by our devotion to mutual helpfulness.

ARTICLE I
Name

The name of this organization shall be the AMERICAN LEGION.

ARTICLE II
Membership

All persons shall be eligible to membe rship in this organization who w ere in the Military, Navy or Marine service of the United States during the period between April 6th, 1917 and November 11th, 1918, both dates inclusive, and all persons who served in the Military or Naval services of any of the other governments associated with the United States during the World War provided t hat they were citizens of the United States at the time of their enlistment and who are again citizens at the time of application, except those persons separated from the service under terms amounting to dishonorable discharge, and except also those persons who refus ed to perform their military duties on the ground of conscientious objection.

ARTICLE III
Nature

While requiring that every member of the organization perform his full duty as a citizen according to his own conscience and unders tanding, the organization shall be absolutely non partisan and shall not be used for the dissemination of partisan principles or for the promotion of the candidacy of any person seeking public office or preferment.

ARTICLE IV
Administration

1. The Legislative Body of the organization shall be a national convention to be held annually at a place and time to be fixed by vote of the preceding convention, or in the event that the preceding convention does not fix a time and place, shall be fixed by the Executive Committee, hereinafter provided for.

2. The Annual Convention shall be composed of delegates and alternates from each State, the District of Columbia and each territory and territorial possession of the United States, each of which shall be entitled to four delegates and four alternates and to one additional delegate and alternate for each one thousand memberships paid up thirty days prior to the date of the national convention. The vote of each state, the District of Columbia, territory and territorial possession of the United States shall be equal to the total number of delegates to which that State, the District of Columbia and each territory and territorial possession is entitled.

WOMEN'S OVERSEAS SERVICE LEAGUE

In 1919 more than 90,000 American servicewomen returned home from wartime service abroad with an altered sense of self that didn't fit societal expectations. These women had served in the Army and Navy Nurse Corps as Red Cross nurses and in the Army, Navy, and Marines as telephone operators, clerical workers, and other administrative roles. Yet despite their sacrifice, they were largely denied the veterans' benefits afforded to male soldiers.

In response to these challenges, American servicewomen founded the Women's Overseas Service League (WOSL) in 1921. The WOSL successfully lobbied Congress for access to veterans' benefits for women and recognition of women's wartime service.

◀ **American Legion's constitution, ca. 1919**
Missouri Historical Society Collections
A1771-00014

▲ **Delegates to the American Legion caucus in St. Louis, May 1919**
St. Louis Post-Dispatch

▼ **American Legion cap of Cpl. August Rausendorf, 1920–1970**
Missouri Historical Society Collections
2001-110-0008

GOLD STAR PILGRIMAGE OF MOTHERS AND WIDOWS

Many of the widows and mothers left behind to mourn chose overseas burials for their husbands, sons, and daughters—a decision that left little hope families would ever be able to see their loved ones' final resting places. In response, Congress authorized the use of government funds to pay for the pilgrimage of US mothers and widows to the European gravesides of their children and spouses. From 1930 to 1933, roughly 6,700 women made the journey overseas.

Mary Pittman was one of the last women to travel as part of the program. She visited the grave of her son, Pvt. John Richards, one of the Missouri National Guardsmen who composed the 35th Infantry Division. Richards lost his life during the Meuse-Argonne Offensive and is buried in the Meuse-Argonne American Cemetery in France.

> Gold Star Court of Honor plaque of Pvt. Ralph Heibucher, ca. 1920
Missouri Historical Society Collections
2007-123-0001

v Pilgrimage of Mothers and Widows Medal of Mrs. Mary Pittman, 1930–1933
Missouri Historical Society Collections
1994-094-0001

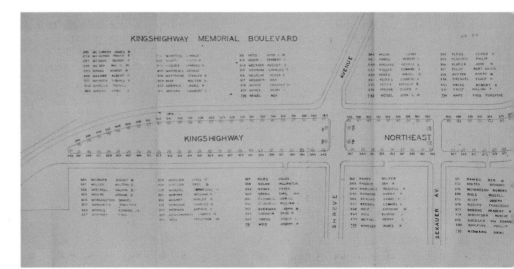

GOLD STAR COURT OF HONOR AND GOLD STAR MOTHERS

In 1924 a local group of Gold Star Mothers began a project to honor the St. Louis sons and daughters who had made the ultimate sacrifice during the war through the creation of a Court of Honor. The memorial was situated in the median of Kingshighway Blvd. and featured a bronze plaque for each fallen St. Louisan bearing the individual's name, rank, unit, branch of service, and cause of death. A European sycamore was planted alongside each of the plaques. Although the memorial has long since been lost to time and urban development, many of the plaques have survived and are now located at Jefferson Barracks National Cemetery.

The national Gold Star Mothers organization was formed in 1928 by Grace Darling Seibold and other mothers who lost sons and daughters in the war. Established to support members and serve veterans, today the organization is open to any mother whose child has died in the line of duty.

⌃ **A pilgrim of Party "L" at Suresnes American Cemetery in Suresnes, France, July 1930**
National Archives and Records Administration
92-GS-1-92

⌄ **Blueprint for the Kingshighway Court of Honor, ca. 1920**
Soldiers Memorial Military Museum Collections
SMX02485

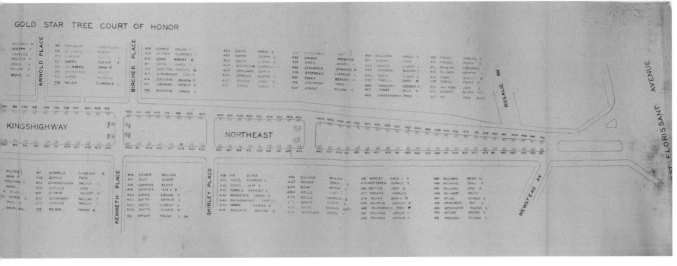

PART 5
WORLD WAR I
TODAY

"This is not a peace. It is an Armistice for 20 years."—French marshal Ferdinand Foch, regarding the Treaty of Versailles, November 1919

WORLD WAR I CONTINUES TO AFFECT AND DEFINE ST. LOUISANS today in ways that may go unrecognized. The work of women during the war led directly to women's suffrage in Missouri. The wartime anti-German hysteria in St. Louis prompted the renaming of streets still in use today. And wartime industry brought new wealth and opportunity to St. Louis—along with labor strife and conflict.

Families all across St. Louis were forever changed by the sacrifices of loved ones during the war. Many veterans were changed too, having returned home suffering from PTSD, a condition whose study is ongoing.

World War I became known as the War to End All Wars in the years after it concluded. Back then it was impossible to imagine that the war's aftermath would bring about a second global conflict just two decades later, one that would call a new generation of St. Louisans to arms and change the world yet again.

THE RED SUMMER OF 1919

Fears of labor unrest and the return of black soldiers spawned a nationwide surge in racial violence known as the Red Summer of 1919. St. Louis was spared from this postwar backlash against African Americans, though memories of the 1917 East St. Louis race riot were rekindled.

The time spent overseas was transformative for many African Americans. Civil rights leader A. Philip Randolph referred to the postwar African American as the New Negro, who demanded equality and possessed a stronger sense of militancy and organization. Randolph's New Negro formed the foundation of the civil rights movement.

⌃ African American being beaten during a race riot in Chicago, 1919
Courtesy of the Chicago History Museum; Jun Fujita, photographer
ICHi-022430

∧ **Opening session of the National Suffrage Convention at Hotel Statler in St. Louis, March 1919**
Library of Congress
LC-USZ62-92218

WOMEN'S SUFFRAGE MOVEMENT

Suffragists decided to link their wartime service at home and overseas to the struggle for the vote. Staging dramatic demonstrations during the war, women reminded the federal government of the hypocrisy of being allowed to fight for democracy abroad while being denied the right to vote at home.

St. Louis hosted the 1919 National Suffrage Convention, where women celebrated the recently passed bill allowing women to vote in Missouri and formed the Missouri League of Women Voters. The following year, the 19th Amendment was added to the US Constitution, officially giving women voting rights nationwide.

> **Hostess pin for the National Suffrage Convention, March 1919**
Missouri Historical Society Collections
1962-313-0002

◄ **Daniel Fitzpatrick's *Woman Suffrage*
crayon drawing, ca. 1919**
Missouri Historical Society Collections
1958-287-0001

MAJOR SIDNEY SCHWAB AND PTSD

Among the leaders in the study of PTSD was
neurologist Dr. Sidney Schwab of Washington
University in St. Louis. Maj. Schwab went overseas
with Base Hospital 21 but was later transferred to
Base Hospital 117, which specialized in the treatment
of PTSD and other war neuroses. In the years
following the war, Schwab wrote about the causes,
misdiagnoses, and treatment of these mental health
conditions.

◄ **Maj. Sidney Schwab, ca. 1939**
Missouri Historical Society Collections
GRA00223

THE MIDDLE EAST

Many regions of the world were redistributed by the victorious Allies following World War I. Among them was the Middle East, where borders were changed without consideration of the ethnicity or history of those who lived there. These moves ultimately led to long-term war and conflict. Thousands of St. Louisans have been called to serve in the battles brought on by these post–World War I changes, including the Gulf War and wars in Iraq and Afghanistan.

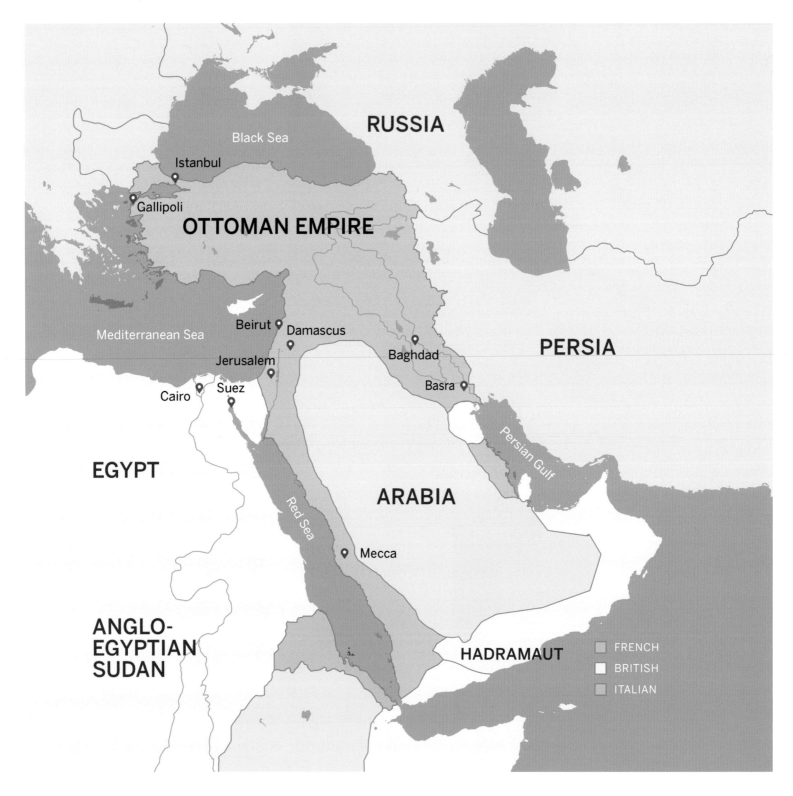

◀ ▾ **Middle East borders before and after World War I**
Gallagher and Associates

SOVIET
UNION

Black Sea

Istanbul

Gallipoli

TURKEY
1923

Aleppo

Mosul

SYRIA
1946

MESOPOTAMIA
(IRAQ) 1932

Beirut

LEBANON
1943

Baghdad

PALESTINE

Damascus

Jerusalem

Cairo

Sinai

KUWAIT
1961

EGYPT
1922

ARABIA

Red Sea

Mecca

YEMEN
1918

FRENCH
BRITISH
ITALIAN

THE NEXT WORLD WAR

With Germany paying billions in war reparations in the years following World War I, per the terms of the Treaty of Versailles, political instability and hyperinflation became rampant throughout the country. In response, a new political party rose to power during the 1920s and 1930s. It was led by a German veteran of World War I named Adolf Hitler.

The National Socialist German Workers' Party, more commonly known as the Nazi Party, gained a majority in the German government and elected Hitler as chancellor in 1933. Six years later, in 1939, Germany invaded Poland, officially beginning World War II. In 1941, just over 20 years after the end of the Great War, St. Louisans were once again called on to serve their country in a new global conflict that was destined to reshape the world as they knew it.

◂ "Warsaw Bombed, German Army Pushes on into Poland," September 1, 1939
St. Louis Post-Dispatch

▸ Editorial cartoon by Daniel Fitzpatrick, 1930
St. Louis Post-Dispatch

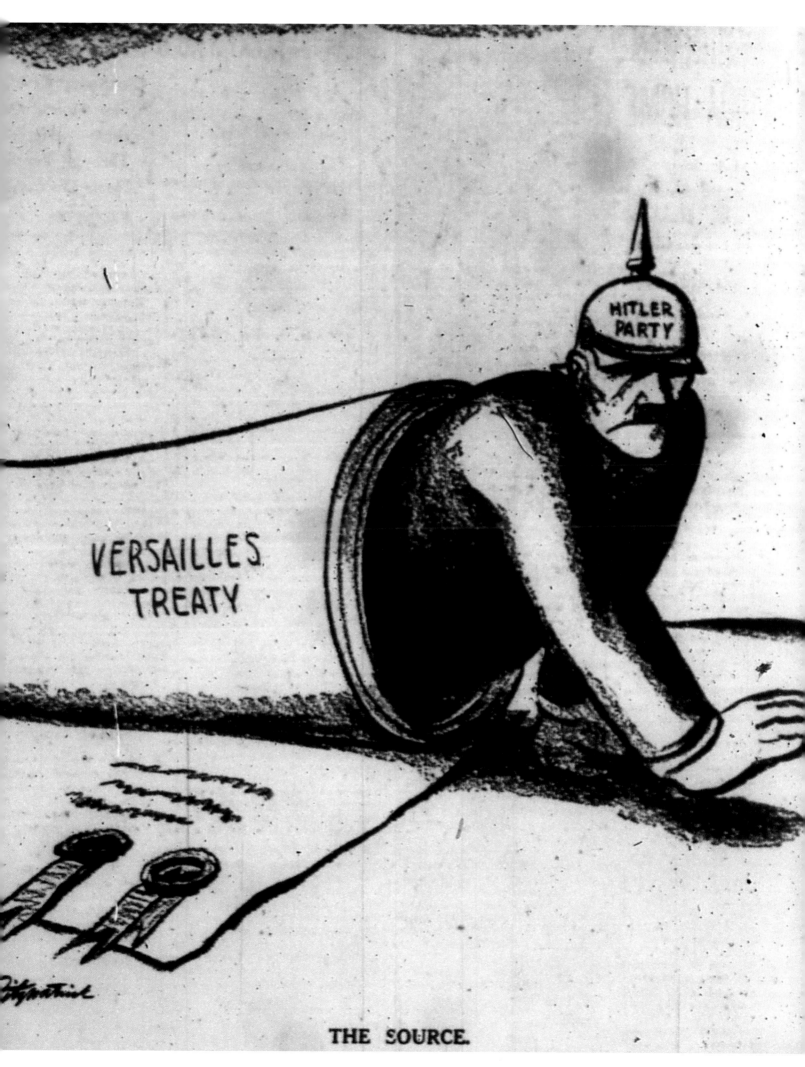

VERSAILLES TREATY

HITLER PARTY

THE SOURCE.

BIBLIOGRAPHY

American Car and Foundry Company. *American Car and Foundry Company's War Activities*. Atlantic City, NJ: American Railroad Association, 1919.

Appel, Sara E. "The 1918 Influenza Epidemic in St. Louis, Missouri." Master's thesis, Southeast Missouri State University, 2004.

Ayres, Leonard P. *War with Germany: A Statistical Summary*. Washington, DC: Government Printing Office, 1919.

Barkley, John Lewis. *Scarlet Fields: The Combat Memoir of a World War I Medal of Honor Hero*. Lawrence: University Press of Kansas, 2012.

Bliss, Maj. Paul S. *Victory: History of the 805th Pioneer Infantry, American Expeditionary Forces*. St. Paul, MN: N.p., 1919.

Broyles, Watkins A. *Soldier, Doctor, Doctor—: The Memoirs of Dr. Watkins A. Broyles*. Bethany, MO: Bethany Printing Company, 1981.

Capozzola, Christopher. *Uncle Sam Wants You: World War I and the Making of the Modern American Citizen*. New York: Oxford University Press, 2010.

Center of Military History. *United States Army in the World War, 1917–1919*. Washington, DC: Government Printing Office, 1989.

DeWitt, Petra. *Degrees of Allegiance: Harassment and Loyalty in Missouri's German-American Community During World War I*. Athens: Ohio University Press, 2012.

———. "Fighting the Kaiser at Home: Anti-German Sentiment in Missouri During World War I." Master's thesis, Truman State University, 1998.

English, George H. *History of the 89th Division, U.S.A.: From Its Organization in 1917, Through Its Operations in the World War, the Occupation of Germany and Until Demobilization in 1919*. Denver: Smith-Brooks Printing Company, 1920.

Ferrell, Robert H. *America's Deadliest Battle: Meuse-Argonne, 1918*. Lawrence: University Press of Kansas, 2007.

———. *Collapse at Meuse-Argonne: The Failure of the Missouri-Kansas Division*. Columbia: University of Missouri Press, 2004.

———. *Unjustly Dishonored: An African American Division in World War I*. Columbia: University of Missouri Press, 2014.

Gibbs, Christopher C. *The Great Silent Majority: Missouri's Resistance to World War I*. Columbia: University of Missouri Press, 1988.

Gillett, Mary C. *The Army Medical Department, 1917–1941*. Washington, DC: Government Printing Office, 2009.

Hall, James Norman, Charles Nordhoff, and Edgar G. Hamilton. *The Lafayette Flying Corps*. Boston: Houghton Mifflin, 1920.

Hastings, Max. *Catastrophe 1914: Europe Goes to War*. New York: Vintage Books, 2014.

Hoyt, Charles B. *Heroes of the Argonne: An Authentic History of the Thirty-Fifth Division*. Kansas City, MO: Franklin Hudson Publishing Company, 1919.

Kenamore, Clair. *From Vauquois Hill to Exermont: A History of the Thirty-Fifth Division of the United States Army*. St. Louis: Guard Pub. Co., 1919.

Laird, John A. *History of the Twelfth Engineers, U.S. Army*. St. Louis: Buxton & Skinner, 1919.

Lawson, Kirstin L. *Unmasking the Flirt: Epidemic Influenza in Columbia, Missouri, 1918*. Columbia: University of Missouri Press, 2001.

MacMillan, Margaret. *Paris 1919: Six Months That Changed the World*. New York: Random House, 2002.

McClellan, Maj. Edwin North. *The United States Marine Corps in the World War*. Washington, DC: Government Printing Office, 1920.

McMillen, Margot Ford. *The Golden Lane: How Missouri Women Gained the Vote and Changed History*. Charleston, SC: The History Press, 2011.

Rumer, Thomas A. *The American Legion: An Official History, 1919–1989*. New York: M. Evans & Co., 1990.

Scamehorn, H. Lee. *Balloons to Jets: A Century of Aeronautics in Illinois, 1855–1955*. Chicago: H. Regnery Co., 1957.

Scott, Emmett J. *Scott's Official History of the American Negro in the World War*. Chicago: Homewood Press, 1919.

Shimak, Tanja L. "A City in Crisis: Kansas City, Missouri, and the Influenza Pandemic of 1918–1919." Master's thesis, Northwest Missouri State University, 2010.

Steinbach, Walter A. "The Lutheran Church—Missouri Synod and World War I: A Study of the Loyalty Problem during World War I and Theodore Conrad Graebner's Attempt to Solve It." Master's thesis, Concordia Seminary, 1971.

Stentiford, Barry M. *The American Home Guard: The State Militia in the Twentieth Century*. College Station: Texas A&M University Press, 2002.

Stimson, Julia C. *Finding Themselves: The Letters of an American Army Chief Nurse in a British Hospital in France*. New York: Macmillan, 1919.

Sykes Berry, Susan Debra. *Politics and Pandemic in 1918 Kansas City*. Kansas City: University of Missouri–Kansas City, 2010.

Tompkins, Raymond Sidney. *The Story of the Rainbow Division*. New York: Boni & Liveright, 1919.

United States Army. *Report of the American E. F. Art Training Center, Bellevue, Seine-et-Oise, March–June, 1919*. Paris: Frazier-Soye, imprimeur, 1919.

Wagner Electric Co. *War Activities of the Wagner Electric Mfg. Co., Saint Louis, Missouri*. St. Louis: Wagner Electric Manufacturing Co., 1919.